WHITETAIL SECRETS
VOLUME ONE

WHITETAIL MOVEMENT

JOHN WOOTTERS

DERRYDALE PRESS

Lyon, Mississippi

WHITETAIL SECRETS

VOLUME ONE, WHITETAIL MOVEMENT

Published by the Derrydale Press, Inc. under the direction of:

Douglas C. Mauldin, President and Publisher

Craig Boddington, Series Editor

Sue Goss Griffin, Series Manager

Lynda Bell Taylor, Administrator

David Baer, Illustrator

Donna M. Wright, Designer

Frontispiece: John Wootters with a Super Buck. Photo by
John Wootters.

Inquiries should be addressed to the Derrydale Press, Inc.,
P.O. Box 411, Lyon, Mississippi 38645, Telephone 601-624-5514,
Fax 601-624-3131

Library of Congress Catalog Card Number: 94-68571

ISBN 1-56416-151-X

2 4 6 8 9 7 5 3 1

Printed in the United States of America
on acid-free paper.

DEDICATION

This book is lovingly dedicated to the memory of my
father, John B. Wootters M.D. (1898-1985). Hunting
with one another defined our relationship, and Opening
Day of deer season was the one day of the year on which
neither of us ever permitted anything to interfere with
our being together.

CONTENTS

EDITOR'S FOREWORD

Some months have passed since Derrydale Press' Publisher, Doug Mauldin, and I first discussed *WHITE-TAIL SECRETS*, a 24-volume series devoted exclusively to whitetail deer — of which this book is the first volume. Mauldin himself is an extremely dedicated and uniquely knowledgeable whitetail hunter. I first met him, appropriately enough, at an airport hotel in Alberta after we'd each finished a week of searching for Alberta's monster whitetails. Equally appropriately, Doug showed me the rack of a truly fabulous buck he'd outwitted just the day before. I had no rack at all to show him for my own efforts. . . .

It was in March of this year that Mauldin asked me to act as editor for *WHITETAIL SECRETS*. This is not a particularly glamorous task, I must admit. It involves proofreading; coordinating photo selection; working with our excellent illustrator, David Baer; and a host of other tasks that I probably hadn't thought through quite completely when I accepted. But I was excited and honored, and in the months that have passed since we started this project, I'm moreso on both counts. As these volumes come to light, I think you'll find that the authors are, individually, true whitetail authorities that we can all learn much from. More importantly, collectively — as each attacks a very specific subject within the broad parameters of whitetail hunting and lore — I think you'll agree that WHITETAIL SECRETS encompasses the state-of-the-art of whitetail knowledge and whitetail hunting know-how in the latter years of this century. And, most probably, for several decades to come. I'm really the lucky one, for I will gain the benefit of that knowledge, volume by volume, weeks before you, our readers, have the same opportunity!

Although this is a 24-volume series, and each volume is an integral part of the whole, every journey must start somewhere. In some ways that renders this first volume the keystone to the whole enterprise. It must set the pace and tone. The publisher and I are both delighted that this book, *WHITETAIL MOVEMENT* by John Wootters, is the volume that fills this important role. In subject matter, nothing can be more basic nor more critical than understanding what motivates the secretive whitetail to move about. And in terms of an author to write about this subject, I can think of none better than one John Henry Wootters of Houston, Texas.

John is unique in that he has been a full-time journalist nearly all of his working life. In truth, excepting a stint with the U.S. Army in the Korean conflict, his entire life. As we all know, he is one of America's most respected authorities on guns and shooting and hunting. And, as whitetail fanatics, we also know that John Wootters is first and foremost a whitetail hunter, a subject he has written about extensively for more than 40 years.

This is John's second book on whitetail deer. His first, *HUNTING TROPHY DEER*, was the first (of many!) truly successful books devoted exclusively to the hunting of whitetail deer. It came about in the mid-1970's, when whitetail herds were just beginning the population explosion and range expansion that we enjoy today. It was a runaway best-seller, and it's not exaggeration to say that it helped shape whitetail deer hunting as we know and love it today. That book is out of print, and since whitetail hunting has changed — and our knowledge of whitetails has expanded — Wootters has no plans to bring it back.

This volume, in many ways, reflects both the changes in deer hunting and the expansion of our knowledge that has come about in the nearly 20 years since *HUNTING TROPHY DEER*. It also reflects 50 years of experience on the part of a very serious, very dedicated, and very meticulous student of the whitetail. I have been very fortunate to have hunted with John Wootters, and on his living South Texas "whitetail laboratory" on several occasions. It was John Wootters himself who rattled up the first buck I had seen come to the "horns." And I have seen the raw material that makes up his unique "database" of deer movement, compiled now over more than 15 seasons. The raw materials, by the way, are the whitetails themselves. And, like anyone who has been privileged to hunt his "laboratory" — Los Cuernos Ranch — I have kept notes as requested and contributed my "findings" — deer sightings — to this unique database that is so important to this particular volume and this particular subject!

With keen insight based on a half-century of experience, and with a genuine database yielding thousands of deer sightings under widely varying conditional parameters, John Wootters is uniquely qualified to share his knowledge on whitetail movement. This volume has already made me a better-informed and more observant whitetail hunter, as I'm sure it will everyone who reads it. I'll be looking forward to working with each and every future volume by each and every author — and I know you share my anticipation. But those volumes lie in the future, and now *WHITETAIL MOVEMENT* lies in your hands. So with great pleasure I surrender the floor to my old friend, colleague, and, in so many ways, my mentor of long standing — John Wootters.

Craig Boddington
Monument, Colorado
June, 1994

makes the occasional success into a triumph. Many still-hunters take a stand during those hours when the deer are on the move, as in early morning and late evening, and turn to still-hunting in the midday period, when orthodox thinking has the animals bedded.

Being a natural-born contrarian, with little faith in orthodoxy, however, I tend to operate in exactly the opposite fashion, still-hunting during deer activity periods and retiring to a stand between 11:00 a.m. and 2:00 p.m. I find that I not only see more animals, but that I get closer to those I see, when I still-hunt while the deer are on the move. The reason is simple; a deer that's lying down, practically motionless, is much harder for me to notice, at least until he explodes out of his bed. And explode he probably will, because, although resting, he'll be keenly alert. Since he's stationary and I'm moving, the odds are that he'll see me before I see him almost every time, and I really dislike running shots. When the deer is up and moving, however, his eyes detect other movements in the woods much less readily. Additionally, his mind may not be 100 percent on security; his attention may be distracted by other concerns, such as foraging or sex. Further, whitetails are hypersensitive to disturbances within their bedding areas, and I hate to intrude there.

Obviously, if I prefer to still-hunt when the deer are moving about, it's necessary for me to know — or, at least, to guess right fairly often — when they *will* move. The point is that, contrary to superficial impressions, such knowledge is no less important when Plan A is operational than Plan B.

Actually, the ability to predict when, where, why, and by what routes whitetail deer will move on a given day is perhaps *the* most fundamental of all deer-hunting skills.

Just about every tactical decision a hunter makes and everything he does is based in some way upon expected deer movement. How to hunt and where, where to hang the stand, how to approach it, perhaps even what clothing (which camo pattern and how warm?) to wear and which rifle to tote, all depend upon how the hunter thinks the deer will react to weather, moon, local hunting pressure, the progress of the rut, current food availability, etc., etc., etc.

Our topic in this volume of *WHITETAIL SECRETS*, then, is among the most universal of all whitetail-hunting considerations. It is also one of the most fascinating and complex of all the studies of whitetail behavior that

"Passive hunting" — arranging to have the game come to the hunter — is Plan B and includes a great variety of accessory techniques such as grunt-calling, rattling, baiting, decoying, and driving.

every hunter makes. The list of influences seems almost endless, literally from the movements of the sun, moon, and earth in the solar system to the local ripening schedule of berries and mast. Furthermore, all these things are intricately interrelated and modified by dozens of other factors, such as those listed just above: weather, moon, pressure, rut, and much, much, more.

Me and My Database

What follows is my "take" on the subject of whitetail movement, based on 52 years of study and field observations and backed up by a unique database correlating whitetail sightings with various environmental factors over 15 hunting seasons. I used the phrase "52 years" to emphasize that watching and learning about whitetail deer is not just a hunting-season activity. I "hunt" with binoculars, cameras, and camcorder the year around, and have done so to whatever extent possible since boyhood. I've been fortunate enough to own various chunks of whitetail habitat for almost 40 years, and have enjoyed access to large additional tracts, during that time as well as the previous 20 years. Since about 1955, a large part of my livelihood has come from writing and lecturing about deer and deer hunting, which would be motivation enough to study their movement patterns even if they were not a virtual lifelong obsession.

From the General to the Particular

In what follows, we will begin with the broadest generalities — annual and seasonal cycles — and progress toward the most specific micro-influences which affect deer movement. I think I can prove some of what I shall propose herein, and some of the rest of it must be regarded as my personal hypothesis, which is a polite way of saying "Wootters' nutty ideas!"

Still, I was the first to propose in print several of those nutty ideas which are now to be found in most every deer-hunting book and magazine article. Others of my nutty ideas are things that a half-century of practical observations have convinced me are true but which I cannot yet prove. In these cases, you'll just have to decide for yourself whether or not my theory fits your own observations of your deer in your own neck of the woods.

Still-hunting — moving very slowly and quietly through the cover, expecting to encounter game at any moment — is what the author calls "active hunting" (or Plan A).

A couple of things must be borne in mind as you read this (or any other) book on whitetails, however. The most important of these is that deer aren't mechanical robots, programmed always to respond in a fixed way to a specific stimulus. Quite the contrary, they have minds of their own, and are highly individualistic, with distinctive personalities and reactions. This individualism is a prominent characteristic of the species. The personalities even of twin fawns may differ noticeably, one from the other, and many does — physically almost indistinguishable — are easily identified, once you get to know them, just by traits of personality and behavior. For at least 13 years a certain doe we nicknamed "The Old Bat" frequented the headquarters of the small ranch my wife and I own on the Mexican border of Texas. Even our visitors quickly learned to pick her out of a herd of eight or 10 in the yard after watching her interact with the other deer for a few minutes. She was a selfish, overbearing, ill-tempered *grande dame* of whitetail does, and she ran that yard with an iron hoof, mercilessly bullying even much bigger bucks (except when they were in hard antler). I should add that, for all her obnoxious personality, The Old Bat was a phenomenally successful mother and raised a startling total of fine, healthy fawns over her long life.

All of this is to reinforce my point that no two whitetails are exactly alike. This means that very little can be chiseled in granite about how deer will respond to this or that stimulus. It must be understood, for example, that a statement that whitetail movement is suppressed by temperatures above a certain reading must be interpreted as meaning that a given buck may very well move when it's warmer than that if he damn well feels like it!

Another *caveat* is that deer in different parts of the very wide whitetail range (Canada to Peru) may exhibit slightly different reactions on a geographic basis. They're all whitetails *(Odocoileus virginianus)* but may belong to one of some 38 or so different recognized *sub*species. It would not be surprising that a tropics-bred whitetail in, say, southern Mexico would, if he ever encountered one, be profoundly distressed by an Arctic cold front about which a northern Minnesota whitetail would hardly think twice. Or that a heat wave the Mexican deer would enjoy would be torture for the northern animal.

Hunters must realize that whitetail deer are extremely individualistic in their reactions to stimuli of all kinds, and that their behavior follows almost no hard and fast rules.

Whitetails, after all, are the most adaptable of all large game species, and that very adaptability has allowed them to colonize an amazing variety of habitats and climates.

Therefore, the responses of your local deer herd or individuals within it to certain factors which will be discussed herein can be expected to vary a little (or even a lot) at least some of the time. Just as those southern Mexico whitetails, living in the seasonless tropics, grow and shed antlers on a random schedule, so it would take different things in different degrees to make them move or refuse to move.

The tropical deer in these examples, however, were chosen only as illustrative extremes, and do not imply that the observations that follow are intended to apply universally. I mean them to be of use mostly in North America — from northeastern Mexico throughout the U. S., and Canada. That's more than enough territory on which to try to pontificate!

CHAPTER ONE

CYCLES AND RHYTHMS

Whitetail deer are known as the most sedentary of all North American big-game animals. In some areas (northern Michigan, for example), an individual deer may live out his or her whole life within a home range as small as 500 to 700 acres. Large geographic differences do exist, however; telemetry of mature bucks in South Texas' brush country has shown that some of them may ramble over 2500 to 4000 acres. Generally, the more lush the habitat and/or the smaller the population, the more limited the home ranges of individual animals. Everywhere, does are noticeably more likely than bucks to remain close to their birthplaces.

Home Range vs. Territory

It should be made clear here that the term "home range" is not synonymous with "territory". A territory, in biologists' lingo, is an area which is *defended* by its occupant against other individuals of the same species. A home range is simply a definable area where an animal spends most of its time, which may also be occupied simultaneously by other individuals. By these definitions, whitetail deer are not truly territorial creatures. Their attachment to their home ranges, however, is so strong that it may prove almost impossible to drive a whitetail out of his own turf permanently with anything less than fire or bulldozers.

This attachment to home is one of the whitetail's most effective defenses against hunters, because it allows him to be intimately familiar with every feature of a smaller chunk of terrain. And, believe me, he is! It may be an exaggeration to say that he literally knows the appearance of every shrub in his range from every angle, but it's not too much to say that he is familiar enough with the landforms and vegetation patterns to be very quick to notice something new. Any hunter who ever tried to sneak a new blind into whitetail country, hoping to be ignored, knows that.

Some years ago I owned a ranch in east Texas on which I raised cattle and hunted whitetails. Like most landowners I put out blocks of mineralized salt for the livestock, always putting them in the same exact spots around the woodland pasture as they were used up and replaced. One block, which I could see from one of my hunting stands, had been depleted for a couple of weeks before I got around to dropping off a fresh one, which I did on my way to that stand one afternoon during deer season. Just before dark, a few does and fawns were feeding in the opening when one of the fawns noticed that new salt block. She literally had a fit, snorting and dancing around and flagging and generally raising such a fuss that she made her mother too nervous to continue her feeding.

It was something new in the young deer's environment, and it instantly caught her attention and made her suspicious, *even though a block of exactly that same color, size, and shape had always occupied that identical spot identical spot* before, except for a week or two immediately prior to this episode.

This buck in velvet in his bed illustrates the influence of the so-called photoperiod, which controls the hormonal responses involved in growing antlers, shedding velvet, rutting, and casting antlers.

This fondness for, and sensitivity to alterations in, home is perhaps the most distinctive of all whitetail characteristics. Its value to the hunter is that it permits him to hunt one specific, individual animal, over and over again. This is the only big-game species that a hunter can assume will remain within a defined area more or less indefinitely, year-'round. If he was there yesterday, chances are he'll be there tomorrow, and next week, and even next year. You may not be able actually to find him any time you wish, but you can be pretty sure he's there, somewhere. You can hunt him today and screw it up, and try again in a few days with some confidence that he'll be available for a rematch. Specific bucks are often hunted year after year, being glimpsed repeatedly in a given area and sometimes gaining considerable local fame. They acquire nicknames and, eventually, personal legends. That all this can be true while mature bucks remain as difficult to take by legal means as they are is impressive testimony to their survival skills!

In any case, whatever activity a whitetail may engage in, and whatever makes him move, that movement will probably be confined within a relatively small area — his familiar, beloved home range.

Annual Cycles

Whitetail deer, like all mammals, live their lives according to certain annual cycles, driven by seasonal changes in the weather and habitat, hormonal changes in their own bodies, and other long-term factors. The effect of these cycles on deer activity is often inconspicuous to the casual observer or to one who watches a deer herd during a single part of the year (such as hunting season only).

Deer movement to winter "yards" in late autumn, and away from those winter quarters as soon as the first thaws begin to pick the icy locks of the animals' prison, are examples of cyclical annual movements. The whitetail species is classified as non-migratory, of course, but there are examples in history where the miles traveled by a deer herd between its summering and wintering grounds can almost be described as migrations.

Food Resources

Changing food sources constitute another major annual cycle influencing whitetail movement. Crops of favorite

No cycle is more influential than the rutting cycle — as exemplified by this fresh rub on top of last year's rubs on the same tree — on the lives of whitetails — or whitetail hunters!

wild foods, such as acorns, beechnuts, and other forms of mast; fruits such as berries, wild plums, mayhaws, persimmons, and mustang and muscadine grapes; mushrooms; and other goodies can draw deer from great distances and concentrate them in small areas. It pays big dividends for a hunter to familiarize himself with the foods whitetails prefer in his own area, and to scout for spots where those items are abundant. You can bet the deer will be aware of both their locations and their degree of ripeness — and the hunter with the same knowledge will be miles ahead of most of his competition. Timing, however, counts; many of these autumn deer groceries are available only for brief periods each season, and a grove or thicket where deer were thick last week may hold only tracks and empty nut hulls today. It's not much trouble to compile a listing on paper of the exact locations of various favored deer foods on your hunting grounds, with the fruiting or mast-dropping periods noted from year to year for the different stands of each commodity. Such records, accumulated over several seasons, can offer invaluable predictions about where the deer may be found at different times in the future. Be aware, however, that these wild crops vary in abundance quite widely from year to year. Oaks seem to produce heavy acorn crops, for example, about every third year, and even this varies according to amount and timing of rainfall.

Domestic apple and pear trees growing wild on old farms or abandoned orchards or around vanished homesteads are examples of annual-cyclical attractions. Agricultural crops, however, may or may not fit into this category. If always planted on the same schedule and never delayed by drought or other natural factors, field crops may be considered cyclical causes of whitetail movement. But such crops are often rotated, with certain fields lying fallow some years, and their attraction to deer is occasional, rather than truly cyclical. They certainly do move deer around, however, and the farmer can usually give you a pretty good idea of when they may ripen or otherwise become most attractive to deer.

The Photoperiod

Of all the cyclical events on the whitetail calendar, none is more reliable or dramatic than the rut. I'll devote the whole of Chapter Seven to this topic, but it deserves a place here, as well. The reason is that the rut is actually timed and controlled by changes in the so-called photoperiod, which is a four-dollar word referring to the changing length of the daylight period as the seasons advance. The length of the daily period during which the retinas of a whitetail's eyes receive daylight influences the activity of a gland, the pineal, buried at the base of the brain, which, in turn, controls levels in the bloodstream of various hormones. One of these, the male hormone testosterone, controls the annual cycle of antler growth, velvet shedding, sperm production, dominance and courtship behaviors, and antler shedding in bucks. Actual mating is, as usual, up to the *female* segment of the herd . . . and it is also controlled by hormones and, ultimately, physiological response to changes in the photoperiod. The photoperiod, in turn, reflects the astronomical movements of the earth, sun, and moon, and nothing can be more *cyclical* than that!

Short-Term Cycles

Most of the influences mentioned so far, being annual or seasonal, are responsible for *long*-term cycles in whitetail movements and they are important to an overall understanding of how deer live their lives. They may not, however, be especially useful in short-term planning of one's hunting time.

A shed antler lying amid the litter on the forest floor typifies the annual cycles affecting deer behavior.

A prominent example of a *short*-term cycle which is crucial to that enterprise is the lunar cycle. We will devote Chapter Six to theories about how and why the moon affects deer movement, but for now it's enough to say that every experienced hunter I've ever known has considered the moon important to his hunting plans. I've often said that the best time to go deer hunting is whenever you can, but it's still true that, if you have a choice, hunt during the dark of the moon.

As a matter more of curiosity than practical application, it's worth noting that another lunar cycle appears in the whitetail lifestyle: the intervals between the recurring estrus periods of whitetail does average about 28 days, if not interrupted by conception. This fact suggests that rutting mini-peaks may be apparent about one month before and one month after the main rutting pulse or peak in your hunting area. These mini-peaks, or false ruts, create a disproportionate amount of deer movement, at least locally. Bucks will be seen trailing, tending, fighting, and engaging in a great deal of frantic dashing hither and thither, without much result, and it will all be over in about 48 hours. This activity is spotty and local and may not be visible at all in some areas, but, where it does occur, it's often as exciting at the main rut itself.

Individual Periodicity

There is much campfire chatter about the regular appearance of deer in the same place at somewhat regular intervals. The interval is estimated at anywhere from 24 hours to a week, with more hunters, perhaps, opting for a two- or three-day cycle. If there is any periodicity to a whitetail's movements, it seems to me that it will surely not be during the rut or when hunters are in the woods, those influences being randomly disruptive of any routine. Even in south Texas, where mature bucks may range over thousands of acres, they would not require a week, or even three days, to cover a regular beat around their home ranges. Bucks I've been able to see repeatedly have most often appeared in the same place at about the same time at intervals of approximately one day. More about this later.

Sometimes they are eerily precise. I've watched the same buck cross a south Texas *sendero* (a raw dirt lane bulldozed through the brush) within 50 yards of the same place and within 30 minutes of the same hour every day for four days straight. So far, so good; his personal periodicity would seem to have been well established . . . but then he vanished and I never again saw that buck cross that particular *sendero!*

Sometimes it works the other way around, and a buck is collected, instead of spared, because he broke his established pattern. One such was Bigfoot. We knew he regularly crossed a sandy woods road, but for years we never saw him in the flesh. We knew him only by his track, which was so large and deep that it earned the animal his nickname. Fresh tracks could be found almost every morning, proving that he crossed the road during the night. In those days (the '50s) we had no way of knowing the hour of his passing, but we hunted there at dawn almost every day, hoping to catch him coming home a little late.

Had Bigfoot stuck to his schedule, he might have lived forever, but on a bitter cold day after Christmas in 1959 he ambled across that road, for reasons known only to himself, at 10:00 in the morning and found a hunter named A. W. shivering miserably beside a tiny fire of sticks. A. W. picked up his rifle, stepped across his fire to get a better view, and shot Bigfoot dead in his over-sized tracks.

The buck's body matched his footprints, by the way; field-dressed, he was 40 percent heavier than the average mature buck in those parts and he was the heaviest buck we ever harvested on that ranch in more than 25 years. He was very old, however, and his rack proved disappointing for such a big-bodied animal.

Sometimes it's too easy. More than once, I've noticed a buck in a certain place at a certain time of day and slipped in a day or two later, only to have him walk into my sights almost as though we had an appointment. A few such experiences can — almost, but not quite — convince me that deer really do travel a circuit and

This fine Michigan buck is of a different subspecies with quite different behavior patterns from those in the author's home state of Texas.

appear on some sort of schedule. In 1992 I spent two full weeks trying to pattern the only true 7x7 typical 14-pointer I've ever seen in the wild on his crossings of a ranch road. Had I succeeded, he might have been the highest-scoring buck I've taken. He was seen seven times during that fortnight, not always by me but always within a quarter-mile stretch of road and always between 11:00 a.m. and 1:00 p.m., with most sightings closer to one o'clock. Naturally, we called him "the One O'Clock Buck". With a "book" as tight as that on a buck, you'd think it wouldn't be too tough to nail him, but I could never do it. Knowing where and when a buck has been sighted before is better than nothing, but it's not necessarily enough to begin planning the taxidermy pose! He was not the first, nor, I hope, will he be the last buck I ever meet that I cannot take, no matter how clever and persistent I may be.

To sum it up, I doubt that whitetails ever really fall into a pattern — at least not one lasting more than a few days — despite all that's written about patterning. Certainly it's possible to see the same buck in the same soybean field every evening for a stretch in June, but any chance of seeing him there during gun season probably depends more heavily upon a seductive doe than on any pattern. Ah, if only it were as easy as the patterning proponents make it sound! We remember our successes and forget the much more numerous failures of patterning efforts, but a few good guesses don't prove the rule.

Getting In The Swing

Despite my skepticism about working out a timetable on a certain buck's short-term movements, I don't mean to imply that there's no profit in plotting whitetail cycles. Far from it; every successful hunter does exactly that in his own way. He looks at the almanac for information on the moon, consults his experience on the timing of the rut in his area, and keeps close track of the ripening schedules of favorite seasonal whitetail foods. All this is blended with a strong dash of intuition and a lot of patience and hard work scouting, both in and out of season. The result is what may sometimes seem to be an almost uncanny ability to forecast the whereabouts of buck deer at certain times. Do not allow such opportunities to pass unseized! Shoot the deer, and then try to keep your face straight and accept the public admiration with suitable modesty and humility!

The cyclical comings and goings of a deer herd — that is, on annual, seasonal, or lunar cycles — are regular but still arcane, more easily deduced than observed. These useful, dependable cycles affect all age groups and both sexes in the deer herd, perhaps to varying degrees. For example, an attractive agricultural field may produce mostly sightings of does, fawns, and young bucks but few mature males, at least until the rut begins. But a stroll across the field in early morning will probably reveal the big, deep tracks of unseen bucks — telling us that they're drawn to the field just like the does, only not during daylight.

When Cycles Fail

Do the cycles ever change, or fail completely? Well, the sun and the moon never fail to perform on schedule, and the seasons continue to roll around the calendar. Any almanac can tell us accurately which days of the year will be the longest and shortest. Worldwide weather patterns can and do change, however, and El Niños come and go. Crops — both natural and agricultural — can vary in timing and abundance from year to year or even fail completely. This can alter the rhythms of the whitetails in obvious ways.

Lean years, however, are not necessarily unfavorable for hunters. In lush seasons with seemingly inexhaustible supplies of mast, the bucks have no reason to move around much before the rut starts, and they tend to stick to heavy cover during the daylight hours. They're present, but sightings from fixed stands will be fewer than normal. In years with no acorns, however, or when the winter oats fail, the deer must hustle day and night

If whitetails really are "creatures of habit" in more than the most casual sense, the author has not been able to detect that fact.

to find enough to eat, and can be seen more often. Likewise, in dry years in which the summer growth of annual ground covers is sparse, the animals are more visible simply because there's less undergrowth to hide them. "It's an ill wind" . . . and all that stuff!

Likewise, radically unseasonable local weather can alter deer behavior, perhaps driving the herd to its winter yards earlier than normal or forcing more movement to find enough to eat. Deer are quite sensitive to barometric changes (although we don't yet understand how they sense them in advance), so unusual fall and winter storms can suppress movement or drive the animals to hole up in protected pockets, even where no deep snow occurs. I locate these pockets in springtime by looking for shed antlers; where the bucks take refuge from unusual or severe weather in autumn is also generally where they hang out during the normal hard weather of late winter — and that's where they tend to be when their antlers drop.

But notice that these cycle-breaking events are always anomalies in weather patterns, temporary abnormalities which seldom persist more than a few days, and, except for the exceptional drought, never for a whole year. They require, in other words, no long-term readjustments in your own thinking or hunting patterns, and they do not invalidate all your past observations, notes, and scouting.

CHAPTER TWO

MOTIVES AND MANNERS

As a boy, I attended a sort of deer-hunting academy in Uncle Dick Fonville's ramshackle Sandy Creek camp in Colorado County, Texas, of which my father was a member. The professors with tenure were fine old sportsmen like Fonville and his nephew, Palmer "Peg" Melton. They were veteran hunters and experts according to the existing body of whitetail knowledge of that day, and they were sharp observers. They taught me, among other things, to watch and ponder what I saw, and to strive to reach my own conclusions about deer behavior. Most of what I learned in that idyllic woodland school on the live oak prairie was gospel. But not all of it.

Creatures of Habit?

For instance, I was solemnly informed that whitetails are "creatures of habit," and I accepted this as a fact for the first 20 years or so of my hunting career. None of my mentors went much farther than that, however, with any very positive statements about how this alleged habitualness manifests itself. As mentioned in the previous chapter, there was disagreement about the intervals at which any one deer might be expected to show up "habitually" at a certain time and place.

This Texas camp — pictured here in 1947 — was the "deer hunting academy" in which the author studied as a teenager under "Professors" Palmer Melton (third from left) and Richard Fonville (far right, back to camera).

The consensus seemed to be that a buck makes his rounds every 24 hours, and that if he's seen at a certain place on one day, he'll most likely be there again at about the same time next day. That wide-antlered 10-pointer whose demise I recounted in the Introduction would seem to support this theory, as would another big 10-pointer of my acquaintance 30 years earlier.

This one lived in the hardwood forest of eastern Texas and one afternoon he pranced out in front of a hunter from our camp, who promptly had at him with a .30-30. The deer staggered and seemed to drop to his front knees, but recovered and was away into the yaupon thickets before another round could be chambered. A search revealed no blood or bullet-cut hair, but did turn up the last fork of a buck's antler, lying amid the autumn leaves. The hunter brought this forlorn trophy back to camp to show that he hadn't missed an easy shot completely. The following afternoon, that same man's wife hunted the same stand, and she shot and killed a fine buck. Sure enough, the last few inches of one antler beam were missing, and — sure enough! — the broken fragment back in camp matched perfectly. That hard-headed buck not only returned to the same place at about the same time the next day, but did so even after having had part of his rack shot away and probably acquiring a real Excedrin headache there!

Such persistence seems to make a case for the "creature of habit" hypothesis, but I could literally fill the rest of this book with stories of bucks that were seen in a certain spot, were not spooked or disturbed . . . and were never seen there again!

Are they creatures of habit? Well, to the extent that that all living things get into the "habit" of eating, drinking, and sleeping, I suppose so. We know that whitetails' typical home ranges are surprisingly small for so mobile an animal, which means that a deer visiting the various seasonal food sources within that range will probably appear in certain places fairly regularly. He or she may even appear in the exact same spot day after day for several days running.

Likewise, whitetails tend to go to water more often in late morning and late afternoon than at other times of day, and in dry country might be hunted with some success at isolated waterholes at those hours. Be aware, though, that an old buck will always know about every hidden seep and tiny rainfall catchment that's holding water anywhere in his range, and will utilize the last drop from those sources before exposing himself near larger ponds or lakes.

I may be splitting semantic hairs, but such sightings of deer near food and water do not seem to me to reflect the

Whitetail movement is rarely random; it has a specific starting point, a clear-cut destination, and a purpose (in this picture, foraging for the does and chasing girls for the buck). The hunter's job is to predict all three.

impulse of habit alone. The animals are where they are because they become hungry or thirsty on a recurring basis and those are the places they go to satisfy their needs, rather than because of some aimless urge to walk along this trail at that time of day. I therefore conclude that sheer force of habit is not one of the things that can be said to make whitetails move.

Movement Never Random

I'm convinced that deer never behave randomly, that they always have a reason for whatever they do and wherever they go. It is usually difficult and sometimes impossible for a mere human to fathom all these motivations, but the more closely you observe the movements of a whitetail herd, the more you will come to see the logic in them.

As you watch, ask yourself "why" about the location, direction, and actions of every deer you see in the woods, at any time of year. If he's stationary, what is it about his location that he likes — or what's making him lie low? If he's on the move, where's he headed and for what? Remember, he isn't traveling just to see new country! Speculate. Form theories that could explain your observations, and then watch for actions which tend either to support or conflict with your theories. That's the so-called scientific method, applied to deer hunting. A hunter serious enough about the sport to be reading this very profound book probably never sees a deer in the woods — of any shape, size, sex, or age, at any season — about which he says to himself only, "What a nice-looking deer!" For our kind of hunter, every sighting is a data bit, another piece in the puzzle of deer behavior. We see a deer and think, "Hmmm? I wonder where she's going . . . I wonder what he's up to!"

When watching nearby does feeding from a stand, for instance, it doesn't satisfy me just to sit quietly and hope the bucks will show up soon. Instead, I try to learn something of value from the does. I may use my binoculars to see exactly which specific plants they're browsing, so that I can go to that spot later, when I leave the stand, and positively identify the foodstuff that attracted them. This is one reason I often carry highest-quality 10X binoculars even when hunting in thick woods. In this way I learn not only what whitetails eat in my hunting areas, in general terms, but which exact forbs and browse they actually prefer at different stages of the season.

In the same way, I'm constantly analyzing every deer body motion and reaction I see. What does that mean? Is

Food is the number-one motive for deer movement, and a hunter who doesn't know — or can't recognize — the preferred, seasonal whitetail foods in his area is handicapped. This buck is browsing a species of Bumelia shrub, a highly nutritious local favorite.

it a signal? Does it express a mood or an emotion? Is he reacting to something I can't see? In this way I've learned, as you can, to understand the very complex and subtle whitetail body language almost as readily as you can take my meaning from these printed words. It's all a result of curiosity, observation, speculation, and never being satisfied by somebody else's explanations.

No, not even mine!

Motives for Movement

Food and water are fundamental necessities of life, and, as such, are two of the most potent reasons for wildlife movement. There are many others. Deer look for safety, from whatever they perceive as threats, especially hunters and other predators, every minute. A subsection of this need for security is a fondness for seclusion, privacy. A number of different non-survival-related activities, such as fawning and growing antlers, take place mostly in secluded spots. During spring and summer, fawns too young to follow their mothers are parked in secret spots, and the does stay away from their babies most of the time to avoid attracting the attention of predators. However, they return to nurse the little ones five to eight times daily. Since the does never stray out of earshot of the fawns' hiding places, these trips are short, but when the woods are full of little spotted baby deer they do add up to a good deal of movement.

Deer are also impelled to move in a search for comfort; as to escape insect pests or heat, or to find shelter from bad weather. Temporary changes in agricultural land use, such as livestock grazing rotations, can move deer around, too. Whitetails go to some pains to avoid sharing quarters with cattle, but often flock into the pastures from which livestock have just been removed. Some movements are more or less built into the social fabric of a deer herd, as in the case of the one-way dispersal journeys of yearling bucks or the prowling of mature bucks during the rut. We shall discuss all these motives for moving, as well as the manner in which whitetails respond.

Food and Water

If you asked American deer hunters what they think motivates most of the whitetail movement they see,

In dry country, open water sources are important destinations for moving whitetails and excellent sites for surveying the local antler crop in July and August . . . although mature bucks may not expose themselves at such places during daylight, even in those months.

feeding would undoubtedly be mentioned most. Except in hard times, this is seldom true. Deer are ruminants — cud-chewers — and the ruminant digestive system is designed so that an animal can fill its rumen, or first "stomach," as rapidly as possible and then retire to a secluded spot to process the food at leisure. Evolution has arranged for the complicated and time-consuming extraction of nutrients from coarse forage to take place where the animal is safest; least exposed to observation by potential enemies. Therefore, most overall deer movement seen by hunters may not be motivated by food-gathering.

If the next question on that survey asked the hunter what deer eat, you might be surprised at how many of the answers would be wrong! Of all the mysteries in

American deer hunting, the greatest to me is the depth and scope of ignorance among otherwise competent hunters about their quarry's diet. Some will shrug and say, "Grass, I guess!"

Across their whole range, whitetail deer partake of literally hundreds and hundreds of different species of plant foods (of which grass represents a percentage ranging from none to negligible. If you picked a deer up in south Texas and set him down on Quebec's Anticosti Island, he wouldn't recognize a single plant, so different are those habitats. However, neither would he starve to death, either, so adaptable is the whitetail, and he'd quickly sort out what was good and nutritious and what to stay away from.

Wherever they may be, deer characteristically browse on a very wide variety of plant types, but they almost

The rut is the prime mover of whitetails. This hunter inspects a hoof-torn battleground where two bucks fought seriously on breeding rights.

never really pig out on any one species. Instead, white-tails are dainty and discriminating feeders, taking a nip of this and a bite of that and a mouthful of the other, moving fairly rapidly along as they feed and never damaging any individual plant by excessive browsing. Therefore, it's simplistic to say that "deer eat acorns" or "deer eat white cedar;" deer do eat those things sometimes, but, given any choice at all, deer do not subsist on those or any other staple foods. Certain plants are favorites, like candy to a kid, but these species, even when plentiful, never form the bulk of a deer's diet. Certainly, staking out places where especially favored foods abound is a practical idea, but you will probably notice that no one deer hangs around too long. He or she shows up, enjoys the local bounty for a few minutes or a half-hour, and then wanders out of sight, to be replaced continually by fresh arrivals.

A hunter worth his salt should know what the local whitetails eat. I mean, not just the "dessert" favorites, but at least the top 20 locally preferred plant types, and also which ones they depend on at different times of the year. Your state fish and game department biologists or your local librarian can probably direct you to sources of such information.

Second, he must learn to recognize these plants in the field in their various stages: in bloom, in fruit, in winter condition, etc. This isn't as easy as it sounds, since many of the most important deer foods are likely to be inconspicuous little "weeds" (called forbs) that tend to look a lot alike. If there is a U.S.D.A. Soil Conservation Service (SCS) office in your area, it may have a botanist or a range ecologist who can help. Try to learn the most important deer foods first, and pick up on the minor ones as time goes by.

Once you know what these plants look like, you'll notice them on your scouting forays, and learn where they're most plentiful. Obviously, they're a powerful moving force for deer.

Whitetails love water, and most good whitetail habitat has plenty of it. Although the deer can and do get some water from food sources such as wild melons, prickly pear cactus, and various fruits, they still need dependable supplies of surface water. Today's big populations of whitetails were not possible in semi-arid south Texas until the post-World War II boom in livestock watering ponds (known locally as "tanks") promoted and cost-shared by the SCS. The similar country in northeastern Mexico is just now enjoying exactly such a population explosion of deer as ranchers provide more and more man-made ponds.

Hunting over waterholes is an important method of hunting only in these drier parts of the range, and even here it's less productive than might be expected because of the tendency of bucks to turn nocturnal with even a little hunting pressure.

In dry country, rutting bucks are aware of every place in their habitat where girl deer come regularly, especially including watering places. They often set up breeding territories close to such places, hoping to waylay any thirsty doe who also happens to be in or nearing her estrus period. These territories are easy to identify, with numerous rubs and active scrapes in a limited area along one or more of the trails to the water. The finest buck I've ever taken was minding just such a territory adjacent to a secluded south Texas tank, and I've watched many others figuratively standing on the corner making wolf-whistles at every doe coming down to drink. Mexican vaqueros of my acquaintance have, too, and say that every waterhole belongs to a big buck.

   In dry country, then, waterholes are important hunting resources during the rut, as well as anywhere daily high temperatures can reach into the 90s during hunting season. They move deer.

The Querencia

Many — maybe even most — of the whitetail tracks that aren't made in the rut point eventually in the direction of strongholds, areas known to the deer as places of safety. They rise from their beds and proceed to a feeding or watering place. Their need satisfied, they drift back to a safe place in order to lie down and chew the cud in peace and quiet. When startled, they tend to slip away or to flee from the presence of danger and then to circle back as quickly as possible to their safe zone. In the lore of bullfighting, there is the concept of the "*querencia*", the bull's "beloved place" in the ring, a sort of psychological fortress, to which he persistently returns whenever he can and where he is most dangerous to try to approach. I have *querencias* of my own, and I think whitetail deer do, too.

I remember playing tag with a certain big buck that cleverly maneuvered to keep me upwind so he could keep track of me with his nose as I tried to stalk him through heavy cover. No matter how I turned and

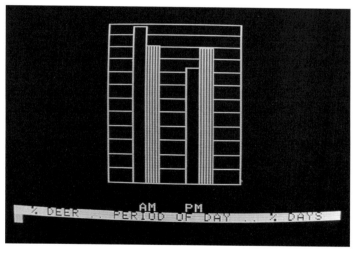

This computer-generated graph from the Los Cuernos Database indicates that about three-fifths of the deer (58%) were seen during morning hunts, versus two-fifths (42%) during evening hunts, whereas the hunting time was almost evenly divided between the two periods.

The open bar on the left of each pair represents the percentage of deer seen, the shaded, right-hand bars the percentage of hunts falling into the AM or PM category. Each horizontal line is five percentage points.

This mature buck was betrayed by the Moon of Love, the mating urge.

twisted and stopped and started, trying to confuse him, he kept me at arm's-length, so to speak, for a good half-mile. I heard him take off repeatedly and caught a few glimpses of gray and white, but never got a good enough look to shoot. Finally, though, I managed to slip past him and reach a woods road, where I was sitting in the edge of the brush as he crossed a few minutes later. I had him in the crosshairs at 100 yards, but opted not to shoot. After he disappeared, I decided just to sit where I was and wait for my ride, which was due in about 20 minutes.

That was how, 10 minutes later, I was able to see the same buck recross the road 300 yards up the way, trotting straight back to his *querencia*.

This impulse to return to a stronghold — a more or less undisturbed place wherein they can detect approaching danger and from which they can easily escape — is a very powerful cause of whitetail movement.

The Moon of Love

The whitetail rut is so important to hunters that it will have a whole chapter to itself, but it's worth mentioning here that two characteristics about rutting movement are unique. The first is that this movement is totally unpredictable as to where, when, and in what direction it may flow. The second is that there is an awful lot of it, and it goes on for 24 hours a day!

The importance of the breeding season is summed up as follows: it's the time of year when most hunters will probably see more bucks (and better bucks) than all the rest of the year combined. I'd hate to do it, but if I had to I'd swap all the other 50 weeks for the one fortnight around the peak of the rut. Unfortunately, these words will not comfort hunters in those states where deer season isn't open during the rut.

CHAPTER THREE

PRESSURES AND PUTDOWNS

Having reviewed the reasons whitetails move (at least, those we know about) we must remind ourselves that, as has been pointed out, deer are anything but automatons. On the contrary, they're quite flexible about changing their patterns and lifestyle on short notice to respond to new influences.

If whitetail deer had TVs, chances are they'd watch Rush Limbaugh. They're conservatives (not to say reactionaries) in that they tend to regard change with suspicion. And the rate at which they become aware of and adjust to any change in the neighborhood is sometimes startling.

A Piece of Cake

A memorable example of this occurred in 1979 on a ranch where a certain 5000-acre pasture had not been hunted during the memory of even the oldest deer then alive there. Needless to say, there were a lot of mature bucks around, with some fine trophy heads. Hunting did occur on some of the surrounding properties, and since the deer could come and go freely, we knew some of the

Any permanently-located stand can suppress deer movement in its vicinity through excessive use, resulting in "stand burn-out".

bucks living in this pasture could have had experience with hunters. But the only humans entering our pasture had been a few oilfield hands, cowboys, windmill mechanics, and other ranch laborers. None of these were allowed to carry guns.

I arranged to take my penultimate boss into this paradise, and a friend went ahead to set up camp and do some scouting. When I arrived with the boss, the scout took me aside and said, with a huge grin, "John, it's gonna be a piece of cake! I never saw a ranch where big bucks just stand around 40 yards off the road and stare at a pickup truck like these do."

There was something ominous about hearing the words "big bucks" and "piece of cake" in the same sentence, but I so badly wanted this hunt to go well that I ignored it. To make a long story short, it was not a piece of cake, despite great good luck with the weather and rut.

Within a single day, every buck in that pasture began to run as though from the devil himself at the first appearance of our vehicles, at distances up to 300 or 400 yards. Of course, deer can easily tell trucks they see and hear regularly from strange ones, but why had these deer shown so little alarm during our first day of reconnaissance? It was when we showed them something new — stopping to study the bucks through binoculars, and leaving the ranch roads to drive to stands in parts of the pasture where they'd never before seen a vehicle go — that the deer decided we represented an unwelcome change and that they wanted no part of us.

It took those animals exactly 24 hours to realize that something new and threatening had entered their world, even though many had never in their lives seen a human who offered any threat, or heard a rifle shot. Not to leave the reader hanging, the boss did get a decent buck, on the last morning, but the whole hunt was not only not a "piece of cake;" it wasn't even a crumb!

The Commotion-Makers

With that story in mind, it shouldn't be difficult to picture the reaction of any whitetail herd anywhere on public lands on opening day. Overnight, the peaceful forests are invaded by a horde of smelly, red-coated bipeds crashing around, accompanied by much yelling and

Hunting pressure is one of the most common suppressers of normal whitetail movements, and must always be considered in planning hunts.

shooting. The normally-empty woods roads are choked with traffic and lined with parked cars and camps, with lights, fires, chain saws, ATVs, and human scent and sound. Even the broadest and most general deer-movement patterns unveiled by your autumn scouting will probably be modified, not to say shattered, when that horde hits the woods.

Even where it's not all that bad, on private or well-managed club lands, human activity is still the factor that most often alters deer movement. It simply isn't possible to hunt, even in the most subtle and unobtrusive manner, without posting warning signals that every whitetail in the area will detect. Any non-customary human movement in the woods, vehicular or afoot, as in going to and from stands, alerts deer that see or hear it that something is up, but human odor is probably the biggest tipoff. And all of us do leave odor, no matter how meticulous our efforts to remain scent-free.

Stand Burn-Out

It's educational to go back to your hunting site of the previous day and examine the earth downwind of the stand location. Almost invariably, tracks will make it plain how deer, during the night, circled warily downwind and tip-toed as close as they dared, scent-checking the spot.

What their noses tell them is enough to make them give that spot a wide berth for a few days. My data prove that simply hunting a certain stand for even part of three consecutive days is enough to compromise the location. If the stand offers a fairly long view, its occupants may observe approximately the normal number of deer per hour, but notice that the deer sighted are now out of rifle range, instead of within 50 to 100 yards, as on the first day. The animals are simply leaving their regular trails and going around the stand, after becoming aware that it is in regular use.

Dr. James Kroll, a well-known wildlife biologist and writer who has done a lot of research with radio-collared whitetail bucks, once described to me the experience of radio-tracking bucks as they move about on hunting-club lands dotted with permanent blinds.

"It's uncanny!" he reported, "They wind around to keep themselves as far as possible from, and mostly out of sight of, all the stands . . . of which they plainly know both the locations and purpose. It's like watching wide

Unexpected influences such as helicopter operations in the vicinity can shut down deer movement for as long as 48 hours.

receivers in pro football finding the seams in a zone defense!"

I minimize this effect, which I call "stand burn-out," simply by having so many stands, blinds, and/or other hunting locations that it isn't necessary to hunt any one of them more often than every three or four days, and even rotating hunting between halves of the property every 24 hours to provide as much relief from traffic and even minor disturbances as possible. This policy has been tested for four seasons as I write this, and we count it a notable success.

If "burn-out" of a certain stand cannot be avoided, it can sometimes be used to the hunter's advantage anyway. Observation locates the trails deer are using to bypass the offending stand. Then I find a spot on the trail which offers a little visibility and set up on the downwind side, either with a portable ground blind or tripod stand or simply by sitting down near the trail in full camouflage. In effect, I'm using the now-unoccupied but "burned-out" stand to modify the movement patterns of the deer. By the way, the expressions on a buck's face when he runs into you on his bypass trail, just when he thought you were still in the stand, are worth the whole effort, even if you decide not to shoot!

One more word on this subject: it's probable that no permanently-located stand or blind is ever totally free of the burn-out effect. Even when the stand has not been used for many months, deer will still check it visually before exposing themselves near it. I've watched deer entering a clearing, where I'd left a tripod stand between seasons, stop in the edge of the brush and stick their heads out to stare suspiciously at that stand a full 200 yards away . . . in July! And every deer I saw come out of the woods that day did that.

Patterning the Hunters

Hunting pressure on public lands changes radically throughout the season. Typically, the first weekend produces the greatest disruption to the whitetails' peace and quiet, and to their patterns of movement. In states having hunting seasons longer than a week or two, the pressure usually tapers off quite rapidly after the first few days, sometimes enough to allow things to get back almost to normal except for the predictable weekend surges. Of course, if the open season encompasses holidays — Thanksgiving, et. al. — hunting "spikes" will occur around them. In states with very long seasons, weekends around the new moon may produce minor blips of hunter presence, as will favorable weather fronts

The onset of the rut — suggested by this big, fresh buck scrape — creates major disruptions of normal deer movement patterns, but only for a few weeks.

and periods historically connected with the onset of the local whitetail rut.

Deer movement will be more or less disrupted by all these surges in hunting pressure. A thoughtful hunter can use this disruption to his own benefit in several ways, however. If he can't pattern the deer during heavy hunting times, in other words, he can "pattern" his fellow hunters. If he has the luxury of choosing his hunting days, he can simply hunt when the competition is lightest, avoiding weekends, for example, in favor of the midweek periods.

If he isn't lucky enough to be able to avoid the crowds, he may still take advantage of their presence. He knows where the pressure will begin — along the access roads — so he knows in which directions it will flow. And he knows when — about daylight; the rest should be simple. He places himself so that the crowds will move deer toward him, and he gets there plenty early.

He should also know that few Americans hunting on foot ever get more than about 500 yards from their starting points, and almost none as much as 1000 yards. With a topographical map or SCS aerial photo, he can locate the promising pockets of cover which lie at least a half mile or so from any road and scout them for vantage points from which to hunt. He will probably even be able to pinpoint the most heavily-used trails and runways leading from the roadside regions into the remote areas.

This whole scenario is very easy to sketch as I sit here in my study at my word processor, but I know perfectly well that it isn't nearly as easy to put into practice. First, it's a lot of work, especially in snow or steep country. That's why you won't have much competition. Second, the work *really* starts when the strategy succeeds; when you actually down a 200-pound buck a thousand yards from the nearest road, that is. Third, the popularity of 4-wheelers and other all-terrain vehicles makes it much harder than it used to be to get away from the crowd merely by putting distance between you and the roads. Nevertheless, it's still a viable way of hunting whitetails during heavy-hunting periods. Not easy, but possible. What else are you going to do — stay home and sulk?

Hunters Ain't the Only Ones

Much human activity that may impact normal deer movement is unpredictable, and must simply be endured. Along the Texas border, one of the most common of these is the flood of wetbacks. (I've called illegal aliens — or undocumented immigrants, or whatever the

Whatever breaks the pattern — hunting pressure, rut, weather, or outside disturbance — mature whitetail bucks are the first to respond . . . and disappear!

politically correct term may be at the moment — by that designation all my life, intending no derogation, and I'm not about to change now!) Like wary bucks, "wets" generally go out of their way to avoid occupied hunting stands during deer season, but often fail to notice a camouflaged hunter in the brush. This can result in some amusement, but it rarely helps the deer hunting.

Agricultural operations can take their toll, too. Farmers are not usually in the field in hunting season (except to hunt), but sometimes one will have an irresistable urge to do something on a tractor on a nice Indian-summer day, and may innocently interfere with a hunter's best-laid plans. After the season, when you've cooled off, take him some venison sausage, have a laugh about it, and thank him for preserving some deer habitat. We hunters need all the friends we can get . . . and, besides, it's probably his land!

I once hunted hard for two whole days in an area where I was accustomed to seeing about 30 deer per hunting day, but on this trip I could dig up only one very nervous doe and her fawn. I couldn't figure it out . . . until I learned that the cattleman holding grazing rights on the pasture had rounded up the herd with a helicopter the day before I arrived.

Again, on public land in Montana I once had a class from the local middle school, complete with teacher, banjos and boom-boxes, arrive for a picnic in the middle of an afternoon hunt. It happened to be a bear hunt, but the kids would have been no more welcome if I'd been after deer.

Other Factors

After the works of mankind, the factor which undoubtedly alters whitetail movement patterns most frequently — indeed, virtually controls them at times — is weather. Chapter Five will be given over entirely to an in-depth discussion of that influence, so it will not be discussed further here.

Neither will the moon, to which Chapter Six will be devoted.

CHAPTER FOUR

PRINCIPLES AND PRIORITIES

It is not anthropomorphism to say that deer have priorities. These may not represent a conscious ordering of the relative importance of things in quite the same way the human mind does it, but they amount to the same thing. The supreme priority of all living things is dissemination of the individual's genetic material, and literally every act of any creature — every breath drawn, every mouthful of food swallowed — can be seen as a contribution that effort. Physical survival of the individual itself is secondary to that great enterprise — but only to that.

Changing Priorities

The priorities of a whitetail deer change from time to time as the year rolls around. Concerns of primal importance at one season are almost forgotten a few weeks later. For example, in spring and early summer, a buck is obsessed with growing his antlers. For that process he needs two things: abundant, high—quality nutrition and to be let alone. His movements will reflect those needs first. He won't walk across the street to associate with a girl deer during those months. In fact, he won't walk anywhere he doesn't have to. Instead, he loafs around all summer with a batchelor club of buddies. He takes great care of his new antlers and of himself, and all his early warning systems are on full alert. His own safety is tops on the list. This will change in October or November.

In September (in most parts of the U.S.), his priorities change at about the time he begins to strip the velvet from his fully-formed antlers. Food is still important, because he needs to lay on a layer of lard against the exertions of the coming rut and the privation of the winter season to follow. Survival itself then may depend upon calorie intake now.

Next to groceries, however, comes the masculine urge to dominate. Now he finds those summertime buddies less likable than they seemed a few weeks past; they've grown cheeky, a little stand-offish and belligerent, and his own mood fully matches theirs.

With the passage of a few more weeks, all the bucks have become loners with chips on their shoulders. Moving up in the dominance hierarchy, by brute force if necessary, has become the first priority. Taking care of the inner deer is by no means ignored, though, and the buck is still hustling chow pretty much continually.

Rut and Post-Rut

When the full-fledged rut begins, however, food drops almost off the list. A mature buck literally hasn't time for breakfast, or lunch or dinner, either, most days. He'll probably reduce his nutritional intake by as much as half during this feverish time, and may lose 20 to 25 percent of the body weight he carried into the breeding season. The priority list is now reduced to little more than a

Antlers have great significance to the social structure of a deer herd, and growing them has a very high priority. Bucks do little else during this period of the year except eat and take great care of their fragile, velvet-clad racks.

single entry, and that one reads "spread genes around!" At times, even his own survival seems to take second place to that imperative.

After the rut is done, the list gets scrambled again. Now the buck is facing deep winter, the greatest stress period of the year, and he is spent — tired, sore, perhaps injured, emaciated, his energy reserves nearly exhausted. He has a few weeks at best, perhaps only a few days, to try to recover enough body condition to survive the merciless onslaught of winter. Many do not.

During this period — I call it the retirement — our buck now finds does tedious that a fortnight earlier he considered the only reason for living. He has suddenly lost all interest in trying to bully other bucks and couldn't care less where he stands in the dominance rankings.

Post-rut recovery and survival are always dicey for whitetail bucks, especially in northern climes, but the logic of propagation of the species demands that the rut come just before the challenges of winter so that the fawns can be born in the lushest season of the year. Thus, the new generation has the best possible chance of carrying the successful bucks' genes into maturity . . . and into the recurring cycle of future years.

Fat Does and Trophy Bucks

Reprioritization across the female whitetails' calendar is less dramatic than that of the males, and revolves around conceiving, gestation, and rearing of young. The does never really stop foraging, because maintaining themselves in the best possible physical condition is the critical element in passing along their genes to subsequent generations. Fawns born to healthy, vigorous dams get a better start in life and grow faster, larger, and lustier. Fat does produce abundant milk and raise fawns to weaning weighing more and having a better chance to survive the challenges of being on their own.

The finest trophy bucks almost invariably are conceived and carried in years of extra good forage by mothers in excellent shape. In fact, there's convincing evidence that the abundance and quality of the forage available in the year a little buck was conceived and born are more important to the ultimate size of his antlers than nutrition in the year in which those antlers were actually grown!

It goes without saying that a competent hunter must be tuned into all these changing fads and passions

A major priority in early autumn is establishment of a dominance hierarchy among the local buck population. These low-ranking young fellows are merely sparring, engaging in a little friendly pushing, but they still learn something about their respective strengths.

among the whitetails in his area. A place visited by lots of does may be ideal for hunting bucks during the rut but a total loss for scouting purposes in July, when no self-respecting buck would be caught dead in the company of a doe. Rattling antlers might be the hunting method of choice just before the peak of the rut, but can actually drive big bucks away just after it. The hunter has to stay in step, reorganizing his own priorities right along with the deer. This is another aspect of the advice back there in Chapter One, about getting in the swing!

Night Movement

It's important to remember that the activities of whitetail deer that we as hunters see are those which take place when we can see, which is during daylight hours. When we leave the woods at dusk, everything does not come to a halt out there in those dark thickets, awaiting our arrival at dawn tomorrow to begin again. The truth is that most of the games deer play not only continue but actually speed up around twilight.

We primates are among the few groups of mammals that didn't evolve as nocturnal beings. By contrast, whitetail deer are quite comfortable moving about at night. Their night vision is so much better than ours that we probably cannot even comprehend how things look to them, but it has been suggested that a deer can see about as well on a starry night with no moon as we can on a very cloudy-dull afternoon. If that's an exaggeration, at least it is not my exaggeration, and it provides us with a useful illustrative concept.

In any case, switching any or all of his activities into the dark hours is no hardship to a whitetail. He can eat, drink, chase girls, and avoid danger with about the same ease then as during the daytime. In fact, many experienced old bucks are habitual night rangers, year-'round, by choice. They move by day not at all, except perhaps during that one great exception to all whitetail rules, the almighty rut. These deer are almost impossible to get a good look at by daylight except by accident or by driving, as will be discussed in Chapter Nine. I can remember two or three really big bucks that I saw only once each, in the headlights as they crossed a ranch road, perhaps, or when I jumped them from a bed out of season, and then never again. I'm sure these deer didn't leave the country; that would be contrary to their very natures, and, besides, sometimes I found huge tracks and other sign that couldn't be readily explained except by the presence of an unseen buck — a night ranger.

It doesn't take much, however, to convert almost any grown-up buck to nocturnal habits, at least temporarily,

and hunting pressure is just the thing that can do it. Look at it from the deer's point of view: he gets run ragged by the blaze-orange hordes from dawn until dark and then, suddenly, all the commotion stops. The hunters disappear and the woods become tranquil — from dark until dawn. During the day he's too busy ducking and dodging to grab even a bite to eat, so he's naturally going to change his business hours to the night-time. If the pressure gets too heavy, the whole herd, even the does, can switch over to undercover movement (under cover of night, that is), but the bucks are always the first to switch, with the oldest making the first move.

This transition is a temporary, rather than a permanent, response to a specific level of daytime intrusion

Dominant bucks are the most aggressive scrapers, and the activity fulfills the high-priority need to establish breeding territories for the coming rut. Here the author examines the battered, chewed twig overhanging a major scrape.

and interference. I'm sure those deer I couldn't find after the helicopter roundup, mentioned in the last chapter, did exactly this. A few may have evacuated the property for a day or two, but most of them simply crawled into a bush and lay low until the sun went down. Gradually, over the next week, they reappeared in all their old haunts and numbers. Besides hunting pressure and live-stock operations, harvesting, logging, and industrial activities, among others, can shut the daytime deer down for a spell. But only for a spell; this switch to night move-ment is not permanent and calls for flexibility but no major adjustment in the basic thinking of a patient hunter. He must realize, however, that nothing is on hold, and that all the activities that would normally be occurring at that time of year are still happening, even though he can't see them. For purposes of timing the reprioritizations of the deer, nothing has changed.

What all this boils down to is that a hunter must not only be familiar with the things that make whitetails move and the things that affect the timing and amount of movement, plus the changing priorities of the herd at different seasons, but he must also be aware of the things which suppress movement or conceal it by making it nocturnal.

Hunting the Nocturnal Ones

Since hunting at night is unlawful throughout the North American whitetail range, the hunter presented with the challenge of a nocturnal deer herd has his work cut out for him. Actually, that term is relative; there will always be at least a little diurnal movement. It may be mostly in very early morning and the very last minutes of dusk, but I'd be surprised if a local herd did not move around a trifle at midday, as well. As to the early and late movement, about all you can do is slip in early and cover the likeliest trails, as close to the bedding grounds as you dare, and stay late, relying upon highest-quality binoculars and riflescopes to help you see in the gloaming.

This tactic normally places one in pretty tight cover, without a great deal of visibility, and requires that he settle for seeing few or no deer in return for the chance that the one you see will be the right one. Success in this kind of hunting may depend largely upon temperament. I did a lot of it as a young man and generally found it quite rewarding, especially since the shooting was usually

A serious battle between a pair of big bucks is an awesome spectacle which few hunters are privileged to see. Those who do have the best possible demonstration of what horn-rattling is supposed to sound like!

quick, close, and at "flying" targets. I'd keep myself psyched up and on hair-trigger by visualizing the buck as he walked down the trail toward my position, imagining him stopping now and then to listen and look around. In my mind's eye, I saw the dew on his whiskers, the glint from his antlers . . . I saw him coming closer and closer, until . . . ! In those days I could sit like a statue for hours, and I could keep my visualizations going for most of those hours. I shot one buck galloping down a trail toward me at a measured seven yards, and several more between 12 and 18 paces, almost all in motion and some of them practically in orbit!

But now I'm in my mid-60's, and my joints get a little stiff if I sit in one position too long, and I've shot 'way more than my share of whitetail bucks anyhow! What I'm saying is that I'm not as motivated as I once was.

Except for a specific animal now and then (like that "natural" 14-pointer in '92), I just don't want a buck badly enough to hunt in that manner much any more. I recommend — and leave — it to those of you who have the patience and skill. Good hunting!

Specialized Midday Hunting

Up against a nocturnal deer herd these days, I just try to pinpoint whatever it was that made them lie low, and wait them out. Meantime, I do like to be on stand at midday. Every hoofed animal on the face of the earth, of whatever species, seems to get up from his or her bed for a few minutes sometime between 11:00 a.m. and 2:00 p.m. He will stretch, urinate, grab a snack, check a scrape, whatever, and then he will lie back down, sometimes but not usually in the same bed. You just have to be looking at the right piece of real estate at the right moment to see him, because, although he might possibly run around a little, the chances are that his midday movement will not total 200 yards.

Stand selection is the key to this game. Obviously, the vantage point must overlook a fair amount of acreage to have much of a chance, and all of it should be ground that might provide day beds for deer. That usually means a secluded, elevated area where the incoming back-trails are upwind of the beds, so they can be scent-checked, and from which at least two or three good escape routes are already established. That is the orthodox thinking, and there's nothing wrong with it . . . except that, at least where I do most of my hunting, whitetails freely bed down anywhere they damn please! I've hunted the same property for 15 years, and I still couldn't draw in all the

Buck rubs may indicate their makers' size: small bucks do not rub large trees (although large ones can rub saplings). This girdled red cedar was not assaulted by a small buck!

whitetail bed grounds on a map of the place. A few areas do appear slightly more likely to be used for daytime bedding at times, especially for bucks, but I've jumped a lot more bedded deer outside those areas than inside them.

The only reasonable certainties are that you will not be able to see the deer in their beds from any distance, and they will be able to see or smell any predator attempting to follow them to the area. Seeing a buck in his bed beyond point-blank range is so rare that, out of 52 years' experience, I retain a vivid memory of the one and only time I ever saw bucks (that I hadn't seen lie down) bedded from more than 50 yards. There were three of them, lying around in the shade of a big post oak on the edge of a field, and I can still recall my amazement when I picked them out through binoculars from a full 300 yards. One reason for this may be that not many deer hunters even carry binoculars or try to use them to locate game, and not much whitetail habitat lends itself to the kind of glassing that one does for mountain sheep or pronghorn antelope. Where it does, careful glassing might show us more bucks than we suspect . . . but I still doubt that many of them would be bedded!

Horn-Rattlin'

Other possibilities for midday hunting when the herd switches to night movement are horn-rattling, grunt-calling, and, of course, forcing the deer to move by driving. Rattling or soft grunting can entice a buck to stand up and look around, even if he doesn't approach. Once in 1965, I'd been sitting in a high tower stand since before daybreak, and had seen very little action. Before I left the stand around eleven o'clock, I clashed my rattling horns (yes, yes, I know they're really antlers, not horns, but everybody in my native Texas where rattling was invented calls them "rattlin' horns," and nothing else sounds right to my ear!). To my astonishment, no fewer than four bucks stood up within a radius of 200 yards around the stand! I hadn't seen them bed down and had to assume they'd been there since before dawn. None were shootable by my standards at that time and place, so I simply watched them. They listened for a repetition of the rattling, and, when it didn't come, two of them lay back down and the other pair drifted away. In this case, the rattling horns could have gotten me a shot even when the bucks had no interest in coming closer to the simulated buck fight.

I'll discuss horn-rattling tactics in greater depth in the chapter on the rut, but it's worth mentioning here that an extremely skilled and experienced hunter of my acquaintance claims that most of his big bucks, taken by horn-rattling, were collected within an hour on either side of high noon. And this gentleman has a row of whitetail racks on his wall that might make you sit right down in the middle of the floor and cry like a baby!

That remark does not necessarily invalidate the main point of this chapter — and, indeed, of this whole book — which is that a consistently successful hunter hunts according to his quarry's priorities and not according to his own.

CHAPTER FIVE

WHETHER THE WEATHER

Are weather conditions as all-important to whitetail movement as most writers claim?

In a word, yes! Few modern hunters ever give much thought to the hardships to which deer and other wildlife are routinely subjected. Whitetails have no place to go to get in out of the weather. Rain or shine, hot or cold, windy, foggy, icy, whatever, a wild animal must simply endure it. Nor can they put on or take off extra garments. They have no Gore-Tex, Thermax, Worsterlon, acrylic fleece, Thinsulate, or 100 percent Alaskan goose down; what they have instead is 100 percent whitetail deer hide and hair . . . and an amazing toughness, right down to the most delicate-looking baby fawns! *You* go out there, wearing only one layer of buckskin (tanned hair-on), barefoot, bareheaded, without gloves, and spend a week in November or December with no tent, no fire, and no bedroll. Then you come back and tell me whether weather matters! Think it over. Of course it matters.

The trouble is that we cannot know intuitively exactly how weather matters to a deer. All we can do is observe deer movement and correlate it with weather parameters, and then try to deduce *how* whitetails respond to various sets of conditions, and why.

Most of the serious deer hunters I've known have kept some kind of hunting journal or logbook, in which they note day-to-day hunting experiences. Weather factors are among the most important information entered, together with numbers, sexes, sizes, and actions of the deer seen. Over time, these journals can accumulate a really staggering body of data, but in a form from which it's difficult to extract meaningful correlations.

The Database

I kept such journals for many years, always eventually bogging down in the sheer mass of information. What I needed was a personal computer — except that such things hadn't been invented by the time I needed one.

Years later, my first PC was an Apple II+, the RAM capacity of which I expanded all the way up to the maximum, mind-boggling total of 64K! There was no mouse, no Windows, no hard drive, no cache, no modem, no fax card, no laser printer, and no VGA color monitor. The microprocessor is not a 486, nor even a 386 or 286; it might be an 86! Pretty primitive, you say? You bet! It still is, by the way; I still have it, and the reason I keep the old Apple is that it can tell me things about how whitetail deer react to weather, moon, rut, and other factors that nothing else in the world can.

I do not wish to convey the impression that I'm some sort of computer whiz. I picked up the "Applesoft" Basic manual that came with the II+ and slowly puzzled out the principles of programming, and then, by trial and error, wrote a program to help me sort my deer-sightings data. My ignorance was so abysmal that I didn't know that a computer can't be made to do certain things, so I went ahead and did them. I'm confident that the result would be laughable to a real programmer, and it's slow

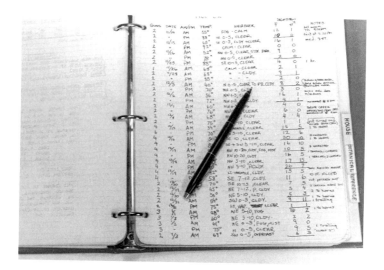

A typical data sheet from which the computerized Los Cuernos Database has been compiled (moon data was kept separately in those days). Every deer sighting is recorded, totaling almost 9,000 by 1994.

and strains the memory capacity of the creaky old computer, but it works. I just can't face the prospect of rewriting the program (even if I knew how) to run on this new super-hotshot, 486, double-jointed, cab-over-engine IBM PC "clone," or, especially of re-entering all the data.

You see, I've been keeping a careful record of deer sightings on our ranch for 15 consecutive seasons, along with daily recordings of nine different weather and environmental parameters. As this is written, the number of buck sightings in the files totals 2611, and of the does, 6231, for a total of 8842 deer seen over 15 years. To enter those sightings, with the associated data points, in a new program would amount to almost 180,000 keystrokes!

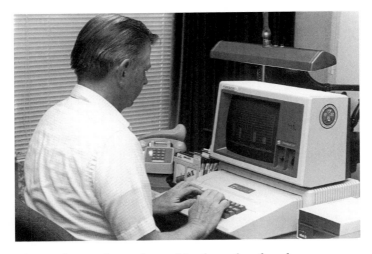

The Database software (created by the author, for whose programming skills the word "amateur" is an understatement!) utilizes an obsolete Apple 2+ computer with no graphics-printing capability.

So I just keep the old Apple and put up with its leisurely operational speed.

To eyeball those 8800 deer required the expenditure of 809.5 hunter-days, including all or parts of 319 actual calendar days, over the 15 seasons. That comes out to almost 11 deer sighted per hunter-day, of which 3.2 have had antlers.

Some interesting number-crunching can be done with such statistics, and meaningful trends — as in the observed buck-to-doe ratio — extending over several years can be identified and analyzed. That sex ratio has ranged from a low of one buck for every 4.3 does to a high of a one to 1.4 does, and has averaged 1:2.8 over the 15-year period. For the two most recent years it has been 1:1.4 and 1:1.6, indicating that we've been doing something right, management-wise.

Duplicate Sightings

Interestingly, although my records reveal that we average well over 500 whitetail sightings per season, the best estimates (from helicopter surveys and other census methods) put the actual total deer population of the property at somewhere between 100 and 200 adult animals. That means that we average seeing each individual deer at least three times during the hunting season, and maybe as many as five times. My guess is that we never see certain animals at all, and see some others many times. I'll also guess that the bucks show up maybe 1.5 times per season each, on average, and the does six or seven times. However, it really doesn't matter whether my guesses are correct; as long as we use the same methods of data collection and analysis from year to year, the *trends* extracted from this mass of sightings are still valid.

So is the data concerning conditions. Each of those 8842 sightings is tied to all of the following parameters: day, week, and month of the season; wind direction and velocity; sky conditions, including precipitation; barometric status and movement; phase of the moon; and temperature. All these parameters have been entered twice for each day on which hunting has taken place, once each for the morning and afternoon periods. The only significant weather factor not recorded has been the relative humidity, which I left out for two reasons. The first was that I didn't have an accurate and reliable instrument for recording humidity, and the second was that when I began this program, humidity did not seem to be a significant factor in whitetail movement. I now regret this omission, and believe that the humidity data may have been illuminating, but it's too late now; there're already 15 years and over 800 man-days of data recorded without it.

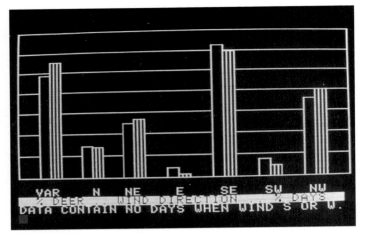

No statistically-significant distinctions appear in the percentages of deer observed in connection with wind direction. "VAR" stands for winds light and variable.

In this and all the computer-generated graphs in this book, the open bar on the left in each pair reflects the percentage of all the deer in the database seen under that condition, and the shaded, right-hand bar represents the percentage of hunting days in the database on which that condition occurred. Horizontal lines in all graphs equal five percentage points unless otherwise specified.

There are other probable deficiencies in the design of this project. For one, it would have been valuable to know during what hour of the morning or afternoon each deer was seen, but the burden of recording sightings and parameters was already becoming unwieldy, and I drew the line there. For another, the exact barometer readings might have helped, but the system used — which simply notes whether the barometer is rising, falling, or standing steady — is adequate.

For lack of a better name, the whole effort is called the Los Cuernos Database. "*Los Cuernos*" is Spanish for "the antlers" (or "horns;" Spanish makes no distinction), and is the name of the ranch on which all this work has been carried out. That a database holding nearly 9000 individual deer sightings made over 15 consecutive years on the same property, during open season, with every one tied to the conditions existing when made, is "significant" can hardly be disputed. The Los Cuernos Database is, I'm told, unique. I also consider it uniquely authoritative as to how whitetail movement is altered by environmental conditions *on Los Cuernos Ranch*. Elsewhere, whitetails will very likely exhibit somewhat different responses, although the differences are most likely to be only in degree. Furthermore, I believe that this program yields results which can be reliably extrapolated to other latitudes, longitudes, and climates, although not without a little speculation and interpretation.

Data Output

One of the key features of my home-written software program is that it answers each question asked of it in two ways. For example, if we ask it how many bucks we've seen on days following a full moon, it gives the answer as a raw number and as a percentage of all the bucks in the database. It also tells us how many of the days on which those sightings were made were in full-moon periods, and, again, what percentage of all the days in the database can be thus described. For a more concrete example, if it tells us that only three percent of all the bucks in the database were seen on days following full-moon nights, that number merely implies a conclusion. But when the program then informs us that only three percent of all the observed bucks appeared under conditions which prevailed for a full 21 percent of all the days hunted, that draws its own conclusion in my mind, which is that buck hunting is lousy on days after bright nights.

Wind Direction

There is a pitfall in such a program, and that is that you can mislead yourself by asking the wrong questions. In the question format, as many parameters as desired can be specified, but the tendency is to oversimplify. An example: if you ask the program what percentage of the deer in the database have been seen when a northwest

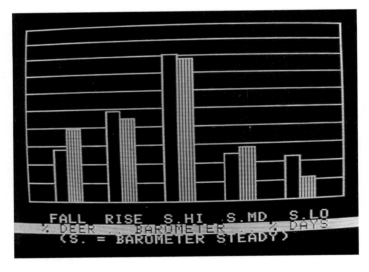

Note that 24 percent of deer in the database were seen on a rising barometer, which occurred on 22 percent of the days, while 14 percent were observed on a falling barometer, occurring on almost 20 percent of hunting days.

wind was blowing, it will give you an answer. The conclusion might then be that whitetails like a northwest wind more than, say a south wind, when, in fact, further research will reveal that whitetails couldn't care less about wind direction. However, they do respond strongly to certain barometric conditions. The tricky part is that a northwest wind in this part of the continent is usually associated with the onset of a weather front, with a rapidly rising barometer. It's the barometric movement that affects the deer, not the wind direction.

Barometer

Deer themselves make a pretty good barometer. Back in the late '30s and '40s, when I was hunting out of the old Fonville camp, the most significant topographic feature of the area was Big Sandy Creek. Big Sandy snakes for miles across the coastal prairie through picturesque live oaks draped with Spanish moss, and along its banks grew a large and very dense yaupon thicket. This thicket was almost impenetrable by hunters and the best available shelter for wildlife for miles around.

We had no barometer in camp, nor did we need one. Whenever most of the deer movement we saw was *into* the thicket, we knew that a weather front was on the way. When the whitetails began to move *out of* the thicket, a day or two later, the storm was past and better weather was coming. Not only were the deer infallible, but they were also very early indicators of weather to come. Their behavior foretold the arrival of atmospheric high- and low-pressure areas a full 24 hours before the U.S. Weather Bureau radio broadcasts could do so. (Yes, radio; television was still just a gleam in some account exec's eye!).

The Los Cuernos Database says that whitetails prefer a moving barometer to a steady one, and that they move about more when it's rising than when it's falling. If the barometer is neither rising nor falling, however, they show a slight preference for a high steady reading over a low steady one.

Sky Conditions

I'll plead "not guilty" to any charge of loading my database to prove my own pet theories. I certainly had my share of theories about how deer respond to weather and moon, but the Los Cuernos Database has left a couple of them in shambles!

A long-time favorite of mine was that whitetails prefer clear weather and that deer movement would vary inversely with the percentage of the sky covered by clouds. This was not merely an opinion, but almost an article of faith with me. If I were a gambling man, I'd have bet a substantial chunk of change that the computer would prove that the less cloudy the sky, the greater the numbers of deer sighted.

Not by the hair of your chinny-chin-chin! I was stunned to find it out, but there's absolutely no statistically significant correlation between sky conditions and whitetail movement . . . or at least not one that cannot more logically be explained by other factors, such as barometer and/or wind force. This and the animals' above-mentioned indifference to wind direction have been the biggest surprises yet squeezed out of the database by the old Apple.

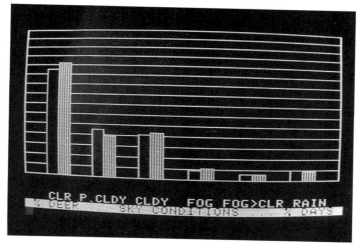

This read-out from the Los Cuernos Database disproved one of the author's most cherished beliefs about whitetails — that they move better under clear skies. In fact, it seems the local herd couldn't care less about cloud cover as such.

Temperature

It has, however, dug up some other unexpected results. One is about temperature. I imagine that all hunters, wherever they hunt, would agree with the general statement that hot weather suppresses deer movement. My computer agrees with that hypothesis, but with a surprising twist. Los Cuernos Ranch is located very near the Tex-Mex border and is distinctly subtropical in climate. The deer there are used to warm weather, even during hunting season. Even so, every experienced south Texas hunter knows that they move better on crisp, cool mornings, and that hot afternoons, although not uncommon, are usually pretty slow. I was confident that the computer

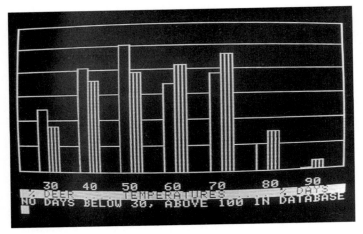

The surprising evidence from this temperature graph is that Los Cuernos deer move freely below about 60 degrees, and lie down above that temperature. Note, however, that activity doesn't seem to increase progressively as the thermometer falls. The effect of temperature shown here probably obtains elsewhere as well, but with the cut-off temperature varying with local hunting-season climate.

would agree that the higher the temperature, the less deer activity, and vice versa.

It did no such thing! What it proved was that there is a certain critical temperature, above which whitetail activity tends almost to stop, and below which movement remains normal. In other words, there is not more movement when the mercury is in the 40s than in the 50s, nor even more in the 30s, nor more yet in the 20s. A more accurate picture reveals a sort of cut-off point on the thermometer, below which deer activity is controlled by other factors, and above which they simply don't move much at all, unless forced to do so.

That cut-off for Los Cuernos deer, surprisingly, seems to be between 60 and 70 degrees Fahrenheit.

(Temperature data is entered in increments of 10 degrees, so the system isn't sensitive enough to pinpoint it any more precisely than that.) This is one of those places where some extrapolation is required to make the computer's conclusions useful in other parts of the country. A Wisconsin deer, for example, may never have felt a 70-degree day during hunting season in his life, so he cannot be set to click on or off at such a level. However, I'll bet that the same *pattern* applies in Wisconsin, or Alberta, or New Brunswick, or Georgia. The deer herds in those regions will have a cut-off temperature of their own, which matches the climate where they live. Maybe a Michigan deer lies down with the mercury rises above 40 degrees, or a Virginia deer may start traveling when the temperature slips below 50. Whatever the exact local cut-off point, there should be one which can be determined by observation once we know what to look for. The key revelation is mentioned above; deer activity does not respond to rising or falling temperature like a chandelier responds to a rheostat, in graduated increments. It's more like a normal light switch, either on or off, depending upon whether the temperature is above or below a fairly narrow range. It should also be repeated that, below the cutoff point, wherever that may prove to be for your local deer, weather factors other than temperature tend to control whitetail activity.

Wind Velocity

The pattern of response to wind force is somewhat similar. Most hunters subscribe to the orthodoxy that deer movement is suppressed by strong, gusty winds. It's logical, because such winds obviously make all of a whitetail's early warning systems — eyes, ears, and nose — less reliable. Therefore, the logic would seem to suggest, the harder the wind, the less whitetail movement.

Like the temperature effect, this is correct, sort of, but deceptive when stated in this manner. The actual situation is that, as in the temperature gradient, there is a cut-off point. When wind velocity is above this point, movement is inhibited. Below the critical velocity, movement seems to proceed about as normal, again being more affected by other factors. According to my database, that cut-off point locally is between 20 and 25 miles per hour (mph). Wind velocities are entered into the database in five-mph increments. I'll bet there's a similar cut-off velocity where you hunt as well, but that it is not necessarily the same as ours. It will probably be set just above the highest wind speed that's common during hunting season. If you live on the prairies of Alberta or Saskatchewan, the wind force that puts the deer down may be upwards of 30 mph, based on my experience in western Canada. If you hunt in quiet country, it could be lower than ours, although I doubt it. In any case, I'd expect that the most meticulous records-keeping possible cannot prove that your deer move about any more freely when the wind is dead-calm than they do when it's blowing 10 or 12 mph, contrary to widespread popular belief.

The reason is that no one of these factors exercises absolute control of whitetail movement. All factors must be evaluated in order to estimate the probabilities of deer activity during any given period. The temperature may cancel out the wind velocity, or the moon (which will be discussed in depth in the following chapter) may negate

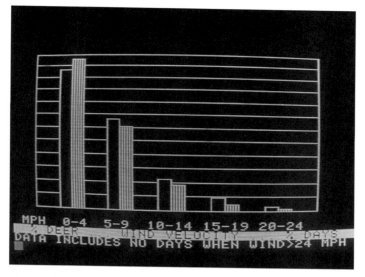

Wind velocity by itself appears to have surprisingly little effect on deer movement, at least until it exceeds 25 miles per hour at Los Cuernos. In windier regions that point may be higher.

the influence of sky conditions. All must be considered as a whole.

However, based on many years of playing with the Los Cuernos Database, I'll offer my opinion that nothing cancels barometric pressure as an influence on deer movement, and nothing overcomes the imperative of an active rut. I believe the phase of the moon ranks right up there as an important predictor of movement. And, finally, temperature is important, when it gets to the critical cut-off point.

These, at least, are the things those 8842 deer in the Los Cuernos Database are whispering in my ear. And do they inform me as to the best time to go deer hunting?

Sure! Whenever you can get away!

CHAPTER SIX

LUNAR LORE:
THE MOON AND MORE

We come now to a controversial topic, the effect — if any — of the moon's phases upon the activities of whitetail deer. Oddly, it appears to be controversial only among wildlife biologists and other scientist types; hunters — experienced deer-hunting laymen — are in my experience just about unanimous in their conviction that the moon does have such an effect.

As we shall see, we may all believe in an effect, however, without necessarily believing in the same effect! It is merely another of the many mysteries surrounding this most-studied and yet most mysterious of big-game animals.

Two — no, three — distinct theories exist. One is that the moon has no effect at all on deer movement. As mentioned, most of the proponents of this view are biologists who say they can find no correlation between volume of whitetail activity and the moon phase prevailing. I have the most profound respect for wildlife biologists. I possess no such credentials myself, and therefore would not presume to argue their findings. I would say, however, that I know a good many biologist/hunters who do believe in a lunar effect of deer movement, but who have never conducted a study to prove it one way or another.

I would also, respectfully, offer the readout of the Los Cuernos Database. Remember, that compilation includes almost 9000 deer sightings over 15 seasons, and it suggests — I might even presume to say "proves" — that more deer move on days following moon-dark nights than on the days after full-moon nights.

That sentence was very carefully worded so as not to imply any conclusions not supported by the database. All I said was that we have seen more deer when hunting in dark-of-the-moon periods than during full-moon periods, when all else was equal. To which I might add, a lot more deer, of both sexes.

What the Database Says

According to the Database currently, we have had only 9.3 percent of our deer sightings on days following full-moon nights, although 21.4 percent of the days on which we've hunted have followed such nights. On days following dark-of-the-moon nights, which have constituted 24.8 percent of our hunting days, we've observed 35.8 percent of all the deer we've seen. That leaves roughly 45 percent of the total deer in the database having turned up on the approximately 46 percent of days following nights on which we had a half-moon, either waxing or waning. It seems to be that these figures speak for themselves.

They are not intended to cast doubt on the professional competence or methodologies of those biologists who report that they can find so such correlation. I would suggest that the correlation may possibly be subtle enough to require a database as large as mine to provide positive results. Another possibility is that their data may have been gathered at other times of the year, and

that the correlation could conceivably change outside hunting season. All 8800+ sightings in the Los Cuernos Database were recorded within the Texas open season, which usually runs from about mid-November through early January and always encompasses the peak of the rut. I must add that my personal observations over five decades of deer hunting in dozens of states and provinces in three nations have given me no reason to question the conclusions from the Database.

Thus, I personally reject the notion that whitetails do not respond in any way to the phase of the moon. They respond, but I'm not so confident as to *how* and *why*. There are two schools of thought.

Lunar Creatures?

One states simply that whitetail deer are lunar animals, and that whenever the moon is up, regardless of phase, they will be on their feet, going about their business. It would follow, of course, that whitetails will be mostly bedded whenever the moon is below the horizon.

If this were universally true, deciding when to hunt would be as simple as consulting an almanac for the hours of moonrise and moonset. I've tried this, and can't make it work. Even after making appropriate adjustments for such other important elements as weather, hunting pressure, and the rut that might override the lunar effect, I still could discern not even a bare-bones tendency on the part of the deer to synchronize their daily activities with the moon. On the contrary, some of the most unproductive hours I've ever spent in the woods have been on afternoons with a huge full moon hanging like an overripe cantaloupe in the sky!

The other major theory suggests that when the moon is new, nights are so dark the deer can't find food, or each other or whatever — and that when full it provides enough light for the deer to feed, sing, dance the lambada, and have orgies. Then, being jaded and maybe hung over, they spend the next day lying low. This concept is at least logical and agrees with most conventional observations, including the Los Cuernos Database.

There is a fly in every kettle of stew, however, especially in deer-behavior theories. Alas, the moonlight-to-see-by explanation is just too simple to be true, and you can prove it for yourself. If you (unarmed and obeying all local game laws and regulations, of course) go out and shine a spotlight or car headlights across favored whitetail feeding areas on the darkest night of the year, you

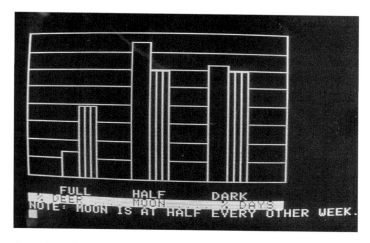

FULL DEER | HALF MOON | DARK & DAYS

NOTE: MOON IS AT HALF EVERY OTHER WEEK.

According the Los Cuernos Database (before input of '91 and '92 data), 32 percent of all deer seen were on days following dark nights (not quite 30 percent of hunting days), while only 7.5 percent were seen on days following full-moon nights, which comprised about 19 percent of all days hunted. Half-moon periods should be at least as good hunting as dark phases, with 37 percent of deer seen on not quite 30 percent of the days hunted. (Numbers do not total 100 percent due to data gaps, and ratios vary from year to year.)

may be practically blinded by reflections from the eyes of feeding whitetails. Or you may not.

Same goes for the brightest full-moon nights. When the theory says that every deer in the county has to be racing madly about, it will sometimes come to pass that you can't shine an eye in a thousand acres of soybeans. Or, you might. What I'm saying is that I think — and I think I can prove — that whitetails move about less on days following full-moon nights and more on days after dark nights . . . but I don't know exactly why. And I don't think anybody else knows, either. There's must be more to it than just light to see by. Deer don't need the full moon for that. Anatomists tell us they have the visual apparatus to navigate on even the darkest nights. The whole matter remains a mystery.

What About Cloudy Full-Moon Nights?

Then there is the question of nights on which the moon may be in its full phase but its light is blocked by a heavy cloud cover. If light to see by is the whole explanation for moon-related deer movement patterns, such nights should be followed by days on which deer activity is identical to that of new-moon periods. But they aren't. I have no data on *nighttime* cloud cover over Los Cuernos, but inspection of the data for full-moon nights which were both preceded and followed by cloudy skies gives me the impression that whitetails still think of them as full-moon nights, cloud cover or no.

Fortunately, from a practical point of view, it's enough to know that the days around the new moon each month are likely to offer better hunting. Of course, all almanacs and most ordinary calendars show the phases of the moon, so you don't have to look far for lunar information for hunt planning.

But there are no guarantees. As I pointed out in the last chapter, the effects of different environmental factors always modify and occasionally cancel each other. The moon phase is almost never the sole controlling element in whitetail movement. For just one example, a rapidly falling barometer can easily cancel all deer activity on the very day of the new moon.

For this and other reasons, I never have and never would decide to forego a hunt simply because the moon was wrong. The moon is one of the few predictable elements in whitetail activity, however, and planning hunts in moon-dark periods simply amounts to the percentage play. Breaks on the weather will even out over the years, but new-moon periods are always a hunter — friendly force. When hunting as an invited guest, for instance, where I can choose any weekend out of several, I always pick the one nearest to the new moon, in the absence of other indications to the contrary. I have no way of foretelling the weather, weeks in advance, but I do know the new moon will always be in my favor, for whatever that may be worth.

Bright Nights Stress Midday Hunting

I said in the last chapter that the Database would probably be even more revealing if I'd noted the hours of the day in which the deer sightings occurred. That might be especially true relative to the phases of the moon. Even without hour-specific data, however, I'm pretty certain that I'm right when I say that on days following moon-dark nights, whitetails seem to be active during the first couple of hours after dawn and the last hour before dusk. This is the "normal" pattern. On days following bright full-moon nights, though, less spontaneous movement shows up early and late and more seems to occur around midday — 11:00 to 2:00.

"Solunar" Tables

The late outdoors writer, John Alden Knight, published and promoted tables based on the orbits of the earth around the sun and the moon around both decades ago

A fine, mature buck, shot by the author on a hunt planned months in advance for a dark-of-the-moon period.

as a forecast of the best hours of the day to hunt and fish. His theory was that each 24-hour day has two major and two minor wildlife activity periods, during which feeding activity and other movement peaks. The only difference between major and minor periods is length, with majors lasting up to 1 1/2 hours and minor periods about 45 minutes. Tabular times must be corrected for the user's longitude.

Knight's copyrighted "Solunar Tables" were published in FIELD & STREAM and other sporting magazines and outdoors columns of local newspapers for many years, and may still be, for all I know. I've known sportsmen who lived, ate, played poker, and slept by the Solunar Tables, who would no more consider setting forth without a glance at the tables than they'd try to fly. Some planned their family vacations around "the Tables," although I'm not aware that Knight ever claimed his charts could predict the active periods of small children!

One manufacturer sent me a battery-powered clock having only one hand, from which one can read when the next major or minor periods will begin, and I even have a $40 quartz wrist watch which displays lunar phases and schedules, as well as best fishing times . . . which agree very closely with the Solunar tables' periods.

I have spent years trying to identify a reliable correlation between the Solunar Tables and the movements of whitetail deer. It would be so simple if we could know when the deer would be afoot merely by running a finger down a column of numbers in a table. Like everybody else. I truly wish I could believe that.

Unfortunately, I cannot. To tell the truth, there may well be something to the Solunar Tables' ability to forecast feeding periods for fish. Maybe it's only my imagination, but I fancy I can detect some relationship to the activities of song birds and squirrels in my back yard. And perhaps the tables might work for big game as well, if their effect were not masked by such unpredictable factors as weather, predators, hunting pressure, and the rut.

But, sadly, they are, and solunar-type charts have never, despite my very best efforts, guided me to a great deer-hunting experience.

But, at least, they do no harm.

CHAPTER SEVEN

THE ALL-IMPORTANT, GOLD-PLATED RUT!

The rut — the breeding season — is the one and only infallible movement-maker for whitetail deer. When the rut is on, nothing will suppress whitetail movement, especially of the male segment of the herd. A rutting buck will move more or less incessantly, day and night, in any kind of weather, regardless of the phase of the moon. He is even prepared to hustle hot does in the face of fairly heavy hunting pressure, something that normally causes him to vanish quicker than a puff of smoke in a hurricane. Excessive human disturbance in the woods can switch some rutting activity to nighttime (when a lot of it happens anyway), but can never stop it completely.

A Different Drummer

Senior bucks fall completely out of character at this time of year. I've had one literally stalk all around my blind at the peak of the rut, knowing full well that I was in it and what I was. I've even had a buck that was preoccupied with trailing a hot doe, nose to the ground, actually run bang into the fender of my Suburban when I drove across her trail and stopped in his path! Many bucks seem almost suicidal when the rut gets really cranked up.

The breeding season moves whitetail more dependably than any other normal factor, and tends to move them almost regardless of weather, pressure, or moon. Under heavy hunting pressure, however, rutting movement may become mostly or even entirely nocturnal.

I said in an earlier chapter that passing along one's genetic heritage is the supreme imperative of all living creatures, and that is the imperative being heard by these bucks. Suddenly, these immensely wary animals, legendary for their cunning and elusiveness, are doing things that we interpret as stupid. We wink and nudge each other and make jokes about the power of sex to make fools of us all. But the bucks are neither stupid or suicidal; they are fulfilling the reason for their existence, performing the only action that biologically justifies their lives. It is, therefore, more important in their scheme of things to service as many estrus does as they can than to survive. Accordingly, some do not survive the exertions and risks of the rut, falling to stress, wounds from other bucks, and predators (human and otherwise). Hunting authors have known for 100 years that, if an old buck is ever to make a fatal mistake, it will be during the rut. I've said repeatedly in print that the highest of the whitetail-hunting arts may only be placing and preparing oneself to take advantage of a rutting buck's mistakes.

The Phases of The Rut

One of the reasons for the frenetic quality of the rut is that the bucks don't have much time to fulfill this annual destiny. The strenuous, highly conspicuous activity we humans call "the rut" is actually only the peak period of the rut, a two- to three-week time when there are more does in estrus simultaneously than at any other time. Depending upon your choice of indicators, it might be said that the whole rut lasts from the time the first buck polishes the velvet from his antlers in autumn until the last one sheds his antlers in wintertime, a period of about five months. Any time a buck has hard antlers, he's able and more than willing to impregnate a doe. During this time, his testicles will be descended and manufacturing sperm, his tarsal (hock) glands will be visibly active, and his neck will be swollen. His weapons are sharp and he is, as we say down South, hot to trot.

The male, however, is not the one that makes it all happen. As usual, the female controls that. For her, the rut probably lasts only a few hours. As soon as — or even a little before — she enters her estrus (heat) period, she

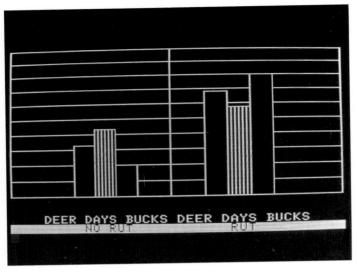

DEER DAYS BUCKS DEER DAYS BUCKS
NO RUT   RUT

This graph from the Los Cuernos Database shows 80 percent of the bucks were seen during the rut, although only 57 percent of the hunting days occurred then. Also, only 20 percent of the bucks were seen when the rut was not in progress, while 43 percent of hunting days were non-rutting days. Furthermore, the effect of the rut on does (left-hand, open bar of each trio) is similar, only not quite as pronounced, to its impact on bucks. (Horizontal lines represent 10-percent increments.)

will doubtless acquire masculine companionship, and as soon as she conceives, she cycles out of estrus for that year. Should she fail to conceive for some reason, her estrus period will end about 26 hours after it began, and she will enter another one 28 days later. In a single season, she can theoretically have as many of four of these cycles, but it's almost inconceivable (pardon!) that this ever actually happens in the wild. For most does in reasonably well-balanced herds, the first estrus period is also the last.

The Shape and Timing of The Rut

A few does, usually the older ones, come into estrus a month or so before the majority of their sisters, and a few come in for the first time, or recycle, a month or so later. This makes a graph of rutting activity assume, roughly, the shape of a bell curve, representing about a three-month period, with most of the activity concentrated in the middle month of the three.

Latitude can shift the rut cycle by a full 60 days. Some herds up north begin in September and are about wound down by the end of November, whereas some southern herds get going in November, peak in December, and may still be swinging by the end of January. However, whatever the latitude, the sequence and schedule of events remains the same.

As detailed in Chapter One, the rut is timed and triggered by the photoperiod. As the days of autumn grow shorter, the daily length of sunlight eventually arrives at the correct duration to trigger the hormonal responses of the deer. The bucks, having already established a dominance hierarchy, are prowling, constantly keeping an eye out — and a nose curled into the so-called flehmen gesture — for a doe who may be nearing her first estrus cycle. Any doe they meet in their daily rounds is "tested." The buck approaches the doe in a characteristic posture, his head lowered and neck extended. His chin is raised, his antlers rocked backward, making them less menacing, and his ears laid back. In this position, he walks or trots straight at the object of his amour. If she does not flee but simply stands there with her tail held horizontal and to one side, he has just gotten lucky. The buck simply walks up to her and mounts her. Quite a lot of breeding takes place in just this manner, contrary to much of the deer-hunting literature.

Horn-rattling reaches the height of its effectiveness during the week or so just prior to the peak of the rut.

Battle of — and Over — the Sexes

On the other hand, if the doe is not receptive, she flees the advancing buck, and he usually chases her for a few yards. If she really isn't ready, he abandons the chase quickly and looks around for another subject. If she's just being coy, however, he will detect that fact by scent and by flehmen (we really don't know exactly what information is transferred via the flehmen procedure, but males of all cloven-hoofed mammals on earth practice it), and he will try to run her down.

A buck will consciously try to herd a fleeing, coy doe into the open, where she has fewer shrubs and trees around which to dodge, and he will sometimes place himself between her and the nearest heavy cover and "work" her exactly like a cutting horse works a calf, to prevent her breaking past him and reaching the cover. I've also seen bucks use a corner in a fence to hem up a reluctant doe.

Once the doe yields to his advances, the buck will tend her, remaining close to her as long as her estrus period lasts. They may copulate repeatedly, but, except for that activity, nothing that my wife would call a "relationship" is to be seen, meaning that he never takes out the garbage or compliments her on her hair-do. He is, however, deeply in love. While tending, he follows wherever she may go, usually at a little distance, and rarely take his eyes off her. If another buck tries to approach the happy couple, the buck-in-charge will try to drive him away — or kill him, if it comes to combat! Most serious buck fights occur when a hot doe leads her current lover into the breeding territory of another dominant buck.

As soon as the doe cycles out of estrus, her boyfriend splits, and begins prospecting for a new red hot mama. As the season progresses toward the so-called peak of the rut, the bucks become more and more excited and active, and roam almost continuously, testing every doe they encounter.

Rubs and Scrapes

Meantime, they're busy making rubs and scrapes to advertise their proprietorship of a breeding territory and their availability for stud service. Scrapes are an important, but still somewhat mysterious, element in the whole complex of rutting behavior. A dominant buck makes a scrape (or freshens one made by another buck),

pawing the ground and urinating in the disturbed earth, usually in such a position that his urine runs down over his tarsal glands as they are rubbed together. Presumably, this deposits his own distinctive scent in the scrape. Just as important as the actual scratching of the earth with his front hooves is the treatment of a twig or branch which invariably overhangs the scrape. He meshes this in his antlers and whips it about, chews and licks it, and sometimes snaps it off so that it falls into the scrape. A whitetail buck can perform this act with his antlers more deftly than you could do the same thing with both hands!

He will probably make several scrapes close together in sequence, sometimes defecating as well as urinating in

This super-aggressive buck charged the first clash of the author's horns, even though four of his 11 points had already been broken off and his neck was bleeding from fresh antler wounds!

them, and occasionally even ejaculating in one. The meaning of much of this behavior remains, frankly, obscure, and even what we think we know about it may be wrong. But we know that this occurs at least occasionally: A doe needs a buck during her relatively brief estrus, and if one fails to find her, she'll go looking for him. During this search, she is attracted to fresh scrapes by scent, and she visits them, one by one. Dominant bucks spend a good deal of time in the vicinity of their central (or "hub," or "core") scrapes, so she often finds a date at the scrape itself. If the proprietor is absent, our doe will deposit her own urinary calling card in or near the scrape and wander off, secure in the certainty that the buck will look her up.

And he will, too, scent-trailing her like a hound, his nose to the ground. As they trail, bucks grunt like pigs, apparently out of sheer excitement, every few seconds. They also grunt sometimes when tending a hot doe. Eventually, he will follow the trail to the lady herself, and the liaison is consummated, providing she hasn't picked up another boyfriend since visiting the scrape.

In that case, if the two bucks are fairly well matched in body and antler, war is declared. These buck fights are not mere sparring matches, but serious efforts to destroy the opponent. Where the bucks are powerful enough, they may literally fight to the death of one or both. In one recent season, I found two bucks dead of antler wounds, one in Michigan and the other in southern Texas, and my famous, gentle-but-free-ranging friend, Bucky, a savage fighter, may have met his end in that way.

Obviously, all these rut-related activities — testing does, tending does, chasing does, trailing does, making rubs and scrapes, fighting other bucks, etc. — distract from a buck's time to do the other important activities, such as eating and evading hunters. They also promote an immense amount of deer movement in the woods which does not occur at other seasons. How can we as hunters take advantage of all this ruckus?

Rut-Hunting Tactics

To begin with, we must realize that rutting is a 24-hour-a-day activity, regardless of weather, moon, or anything else. That means that we spend every possible minute in the woods at this time of year. In stand hunting, I like to sit where I can see the greatest possible sweep of habitat, on the theory that the more country I can cover, the better chance I have of spotting the buck I want, even if I have to leave my stand and try to go to him.

This buck demonstrates the rub-urination technique of allowing urine to run down over the tarsal glands as they are rubbed together over a fresh scrape.

Needless to say, horn-rattling and aggressive grunting are both sounds associated with the rut, but they must be employed judiciously. Loud, fierce horn-rattling, simulating a really serious fight, is most effective during the week or so just before the peak of the rut. Bucks will come to rattling during the peak itself, but only if they do not happen to be in the company of a hot doe . . . and, during the rut's peak, most dominant bucks are with one doe or another most of the time. You can write this down and say I said it: You cannot rattle a buck away from a hot doe! You will do well to make him take a few steps from her side, or stick his head out of a thicket, and that may be enough, but he will never actually leave her for your fake fight.

During the "retirement" fortnight just after the peak of the rut, rattling or aggressive grunting may actually drive a big buck away.

As mentioned earlier, I like to still-hunt during the rut, because the bucks are on the move, less alert for danger and more likely to let me get close. I think the rut is the best time to use a deer decoy, as will be mentioned in Chapter Nine, and the worst time to bait deer (where that's legal) unless you can bait up a hot doe.

Predicting the Rut

To make the most of hunting opportunities associated with the rut, we need to know when it will happen. The rut's timing — or at least humans' perception of that timing — varies slightly from year to year but usually by no more than a few days. I have seen a whitetail herd violate that statement only two years out of 50. In one of those seasons we had every indication of a peaking rut almost a month before the customary starting time! It was an exceptionally good year and the herd was in superior body condition, and that may explain the early peak. If not, I'm at a loss. In most years, the easiest way to know when the rut will peak is to know when it peaked last year and other recent years.

Where there is a high ratio of bucks to does, I've often noticed a conspicuous build-up of fresh rubs in the woods just before the peak of the rut. Then, as the rut climaxes, there may be a virtual explosion of new rubs, almost overnight.

Buck rubs, called "hookings" in some regions, signal where buck movement will occur, usually marking routes or corridors regularly used by bucks. I have taken several fine bucks over the years by staking out fresh rub lines. Rubs are often concentrated where two such routes intersect. In every part of the country, whitetails prefer one or two sapling species over all others for rubbing, and these usually have smooth bark and resinous sap — pines, cedars, hemlocks, and the like.

A fresh scrape is even more conspicuous in a light snow, showing urine marks and the direction of hoof motions while making the scrape.

Bucks often return to the same exact places year after year to rub and scrape. If a sapling survives the early years of rubbing, the scars can probably be seen for the life of the tree. In certain soil types, old scrapes, too, are quite persistent, and we will have more to say about both these items in the following chapter, on scouting.

Anomalies in The Rut

You know what they say about the course of true love, and the whitetail version, the rut, sometimes runs anything but smooth. In some years the rutting peak is a concentrated pulse of activity, as described earlier in this chapter, lasting about two to three weeks. Hunters I know have come to regard this as the "normal" pattern. In other years we see an entirely different pattern, a long, drawn-out, stop-and-start sort of rut that seems never to peak at all. In a few other seasons, the impression is that there simply was no rut at all. Yet there is, mysteriously, always a fresh crop of baby fawns the following spring to show how wrong outsiders' impressions can be.

These differing courses of the rut may result from different weather patterns, varying demographics within the herd, or perhaps even different patterns of hunting pressure. I'm not at all sure that the drawn-out, off-and-on rut is not the most common, perhaps even most "normal," on my hunting grounds. In any case, you should know that these variations do occur and be prepared to adapt to them. How? Well, of this I'm sure: always assume that the rut is in progress whenever the date is inside the traditional time boundaries for your area, even when you've actually seen little or no sign of it. During a couple of those slow-rut, late-rut seasons I've let half or more of the peak slip by me because I was too pigheaded to believe that it could be in progress without my knowing it. And the rut is much too important to miss even one day of it!

Another of my home-written software programs is designed to calculate and picture rutting activity graphically. I call the result the Buck Movement Index, and have instructed the computer to draw a bar chart of buck activity over the whole season, day by day. I include here a couple from Los Cuernos in recent years, to illustrate the different patterns that the rut can take. Technically, the entire Texas open hunting season is within the broadest definition of the whitetail breeding season, so what is shown in these charts is actually the peak of the rut.

Another sign of a rut-in-progress, besides a proliferation of rubs and scrapes, is a noticeable increase in the solitary does and fawns in the woods, separated by jealous bucks and the doe's instinctive unwillingness to allow a male fawn to follow her as she enters estrus. Solitary bucks are another sign, or, rather, bucks running together signal that the rut is not yet serious. The tarsal glands of adult does turn black and tarry as they approach estrus. Obviously, rut-related activities on the part of the bucks — trailing, chasing and tending does, and serious fighting among themselves — don't happen except during the rut. As mentioned, some years these signs are more subtle than others, but they're never entirely absent during the major portion of the mating season.

I have called the rut the major movement-maker among whitetails, and that's true. In fact, perhaps the very best sign that the rut is going is the sudden drastic increase in sightings of moving deer, especially bucks.

CHAPTER EIGHT

SCOUTING:
THE NAME OF THE GAME

Many writers and seminar-givers on whitetail hunting refer to "scouting" and "hunting" as though they were the names of two entirely different operations. If they are, it is only because one — scouting — takes place mostly when the season is closed, whereas the other — hunting — occurs only when it's open. Except for that distinction, scouting and hunting are properly thought of as being all part of the same, seamless process.

All anti-hunters, most non-hunters, and even some hunters (who should know better) confuse hunting with *shooting*. It goes without saying that if shooting takes place during closed season, it can't be called hunting. Call it cheating, or slaughter, or thievery or simply poaching, or any of several other despicable things, but it is not hunting! "Hunter" is an honorable title, and hunting is an activity conducted according to a set of rules and a code of ethics that no poacher, no matter how he rationalizes his behavior, can claim. Without honor, there is no *hunting*.

English sportsmen, who understand honor, use a different set of names for their activities. They call the taking of game birds with the shotgun "shooting," and the taking of big-game animals with the rifle "stalking." The term "hunting" is reserved in the United Kingdom for

Some scouting continues into the hunting season in most states, if only to monitor the onset and the progress of the rut and to check for changes in movement patterns.

the pursuit of a fox on horseback, wearing a red coat, behind a pack of hounds. Having enjoyed U.K. shooting and stalking on several occasions, I've come to regard their terminology as apt. "Stalking," with reference to the subject matter of this book, implies an ongoing, multifaceted effort to approach a worthy game animal, an effort that is its own reward and that occasionally culminates in an opportunity to shoot.

The Nature of Scouting

What we American deer-stalkers call "scouting" encompasses every part of that effort except the actual shot. Scouting is hunting for a place to hunt, if you will — a place where deer live and move. Scouting is searching for any clue to the presence or the passage of a desirable buck (or doe), and the associated detective work necessary to learn from those clues where the animal comes from and where he/she goes, when, and by which routes.

Later on, there will be an entire volume in this *WHITETAIL SECRETS* series devoted to the subject of scouting, and I have no wish to tread upon its author's prerogatives. But in this chapter it may be worthwhile to go once over lightly a few of my personal views of scouting and note how scouting is connected with our topic of whitetail movement.

A hunter's scouting has been successful when he can accurately predict where a certain deer, or a group of deer, will be at some point in the future. That accomplishment should permit him to intercept the animal somewhere along the way.

It is one thing, however, to determine that a certain place has some feature making it attractive to any whitetail, and another thing to try to figure out by what secret paths most deer, or a specific deer, may arrive there. Examples of the former kind of destination might be a Canadian barley field, an Ohio salt lick, a Georgia soybean patch, a Texas oat patch, or a New Hampshire apple orchard. Whitetails love what they find in such places, and visit them regularly. The hunter need not necessarily concern himself with where they start, or which trails they use to get there. It's enough that he knows that they will show up if he waits there long and unobtrusively enough. Looking for such locations is one kind of scouting. Of course, the large and obvious kinds of places listed above will usually be there from season to season and will also be known to most of the hunters using the area. Human traffic can become heavier around them than deer traffic!

One of the things we look for during our scouting, obviously, are the actual objects of the whole exercise, the whitetail bucks themselves! This beauty was spotted by the author in September and, when harvested during the open season, scored very close to the record book.

Scouting a Target Buck

Suppose, however, that a hunter is looking for one particular buck, which may or may not appear in the oat patch or orchard during daylight hours. This situation calls for a higher level of knowledge on the part of the hunter and a different kind of scouting. First, there must be some grounds for the assumption that the target deer knows about the attraction and actually does visit it. Such grounds could be actual sightings of the animal there at twilight in summer, or his tracks in the clearing, if his hoof prints are well enough known to be identified wherever seen.

Second, the hunter must form an opinion — or perhaps only an intuition — about how the target deer probably approaches the area. To do this, it helps to know where he's coming from, and that he will most likely enter on the downwind side, regardless of how he approaches. Finally, the cunning hunter figures the cunning buck will time his arrival near the clearing just before dusk and pause somewhere along the trail, a few yards back in the undergrowth and out of sight, to wait for full darkness before emerging. That's typical of mature, hunter-wary whitetail bucks.

Now the object of scouting is finding the right trail, and then finding a place to wait along that trail, far enough back in the bushes that the buck will probably arrive there while some shooting light remains.

Yet another kind of scouting involved in the hunting of this particular buck is searching out the secret places within his home range likely to draw him. These are small attractions, perhaps only a *Bumelia* shrub in fruit or a few wild plum bushes, or maybe a bathtub – sized sinkhole that holds rainwater, where he can drink before

Game trails ("deer runways" in some regions) are important evidence of the routes being utilized by does and fawns between bedding and feeding areas. Bucks tend to parallel these trails, but not to walk directly in them . . . unless chasing a hot doe!

dark without exposing himself. Only the expert scout and a few resident whitetails will know about these spots, but they hold great potential for the patient, dedicated hunter willing to locate them, figure out when and how they're being used, and set up on them skillfully.

Rubs and Scrapes

Scouting for rub-lines and scrapes, being rut-related, must usually be done after the season opens, depending upon the length and dates of the various seasons (gun, bow, primitive, etc.) in your state. Recalling my discussion of whitetail scrapes' significance in the last chapter, let me now add that a hot scrape can either be a lead-pipe cinch hunting place, or one of the most frustrating features in the autumn woods! There appear to be at least three or four different types of scrapes. I've heard names for many more than that by deer-hunting experts, together with a dozen hypotheses as to the significance of each kind. I myself used to know all about scrapes, but now, after 52 deer seasons, find I know much less about them, and that my body of accumulated ignorance grows each year.

Some of what I do know about scrapes: bucks frequent certain scrape locations and return to those often over the time they remain active; certain other scrapes, identical in appearance to me, are never revisited. Many — perhaps most — active scrapes are freshened only at night, and the buck is seldom seen around them in daylight. When bucks do revisit scrapes by day, they often scent-check them from the downwind side instead of actually going to them. Setting up too close, as for bowhunting, may allow the scraper accidentally to pass behind and downwind of the hunter and be warned. Serious scrape locations rarely have only one scrape; clusters of scrapes close together seem to be more common. Scrapes are quite often reopened in exactly the same spot season after season, and these sites do not reveal to a human the reason for their extraordinary appeal. It doesn't have to be the same buck each year, either; I've shot a buck at his scrape and had the eerie experience of finding the identical scrape opened the following season, as though by a ghost buck.

"Hot Spots"

Sometimes a sort of rutting frenzy seems to occur in a certain area, of perhaps 50 acres. I have actually counted

The author inspects a whitetail's bed (note oval area of flattened grass) in August. He hunts for bed grounds in summertime, and stays out of them during the hunting season when disturbances may make deer vacate for a few days or weeks.

over 100 scrapes in one of these "hot spots." That one also held four places where bucks had recently done battle. I have no explanation for hot spots, although I can offer a couple of theories. One is that they occur where the home ranges of three or four dominant bucks happen to overlap, increasing the occupants' sense of breeding competition and stimulating extra scraping. Another is that a single hot doe hung out on that corner for a spell, before most of the other does came into estrus, and attracted a shoal of bucks and stirred up competition. I incline to the latter theory. Take your choice, or offer a more plausible theory.

Bucks do share scrapes, sometimes standing in line to freshen the same one. Readers of my 1977 book *HUNTING TROPHY DEER* (now out of print) will notice that this is a major revision in my expert opinion about this scrape business. That's what expert opinions are for.

Where to Find Scrapes

Everywhere I've ever hunted whitetails during the rut, scrapes tend to occur in or very near openings (natural or otherwise), along entry trails, and around the edges of isolated mottes or islands of brush or individual trees with branches hanging near the ground. True breeding scrapes, as mentioned, are always overhung by a small limb which shows signs of considerable abuse. Often stripped of leaves or broken, the overhanging limb is one of the easiest ways to spot scrape locations at a distance, especially where the tree may have green foliage during the rut. The buck snaps it, leaving it dangling, and when the leaves die it hangs like a reddish-brown flag pointing down at the scrape.

This chapter is more about finding scrapes than hunting them, but I cannot resist adding that you can waste a whole rut hunting the wrong scrape. Don't be stubborn; if the scrape doesn't pay off pretty quickly (24 hours or less), I go looking for a more active location. Also in passing, I do not utilize mock scrapes in my own hunting, but that is because I have no trouble finding real ones. I have experimented with mock scrapes with success, and would probably use the method if my hunting were confined to a very small plot of land on which no real live buck happened to make a real live scrape.

When to Scout

Back to scouting. Living in the Southwest as I do, my favorite time of the year for scouting is late winter and spring, from the day the hunting season closes until the onset of hot summer. In regions buried under deep snow

at this time, I'd have to wait until most of the snow was gone to begin my scouting. Much can be learned during this very pleasant time to be in the woods, and, besides, what else are you going to do, fertilize the lawn?

Shed antlers are easier to find before spring grasses and forbs cover them and the wee varmints nibble them away. They not only show which bucks survived the hunting season, but suggest their ages and size, as well as hinting where they may live. I find most sheds along drainages, creek bottoms, and other low areas that would offer some shelter against nasty winter weather. Those are the places deer are most likely to be found around antler-dropping time . . . and also during the rut.

Rubs from the season just past will remain highly visible during springtime scouting, and many of the larger and more serious scrapes — the ones that were freshened repeatedly — can still be identified, sometimes with the help of the ever-present, battered overhanging branch.

Locating Movement Patterns

At this time of year I do not hesitate to explore and trace out game trails. Rub lines indicate trails used by bucks, and even suggest which direction he was heading. Forks and intersections of trails are likely to be especially heavily rubbed. Wild animals tend to travel fairly directly wherever they go, but the actual path always follows the "direct route" of least resistance. Thus, subtle terrain contours can sometimes help you figure out where the important trails ran, even if deer aren't using them so heavily in springtime. Remember that bucks tend not to walk in the main trails, but to utilize parallel routes or corridors that may be 50 or 100 yards wide. If they run between bedding grounds and known hunting-season feeding areas, such corridors are easier to figure out with snow on the ground. Otherwise, find a spot where the corridor crosses a dirt road, fire lane, or some similar place and let the tracks from the last few days define the corridor's width.

Look for what I call barriers. These are mostly linear obstacles such as fences, creeks, woods roads, bluffs, and steep ridges. All will have certain spots where it is possible, or at least a little easier, to negotiate them, and these places will always reveal a funneling effect on deer traffic. They're easy to identify, and will probably be good hunting. Don't overlook saddles between crests on a ridge; the difference in elevation need not be very great for whitetails to choose the low spots. When crossing

The author examines the broken, partly-stripped limb that always overhangs a whitetail scrape for signs of recent use.

open areas in daylight, wary bucks tend to look for draws and places where their exposure will be minimized while crossing. A strip of trees and brush along a fence line or a point of woods protruding into a field are always favored crossing routes.

Overlook nothing. Note the species of trees and shrubs wherever you go in the woods; you may find a secret honey hole. The more you know about where deer hang out, and the most likely pathways to and from them, the more logically you can hunt. Springtime is the best time to gather this intelligence.

Summer and Fall Scouting

If the spring scouting was properly carried out, not much remains to be done during the long, lazy days of summer. The feeding patterns of the local whitetails will change so radically by the end of October that about all there is to do in July and August is monitor the general condition of the herd, fawn survival, antler growth, and such, and try to spot an exceptionally nice buck or two. In most regions, this is easier around feeding areas in late evening. Binoculars and spotting scopes are recommended. In dry country, I have great good luck watching waterholes late on blazing-hot August days. Biologist Al Brothers, the father of modern trophy whitetail management, once said to me, "If you want to find out what (kind of bucks) you have, just sit on your waterholes in August!" Good advice from an old pro.

The whole mood of the forest seems to change in September, when the bucks begin to shed their velvet antler sheaths. The pace quickens, and there is the beginning of a subtle ripple of excitement among the whitetails. This is the earliest hint that there will be a rut in a few weeks.

In October, there seems to be a radical reshuffling of patterns in the whitetail community. Places where we watched them every day in summertime are suddenly deserted. Trails we thought were deer superhighways are abruptly devoid of tracks. Bucks whose name, rank, and serial number we thought we knew disappear . . . and then turn up again someplace new. This "October shuffle" seems to occur everywhere in North America, but there's always a chance that you hunt somewhere I've never been. Even then, I'll bet it simply slides a week or two one way or the other. In any case, there's little sense in trying to plan your season's strategy until after the

Wootters' so-called "barrier theory" holds that linear obstacles to deer movement, such as fences, roads, creeks, bluffs, etc., create hunting opportunities by funneling traffic through narrow spots, like this heavy game crossing under a cattle fence.

October shuffle is completed, whenever it may be in your neck of the woods.

Scouting "Lite"

I like to stay out of the woods as much as possible in autumn, just prior to the hunting season. I don't want to stumble into some new bedding area and screw it up for weeks, and I don't want to create enough unfamiliar activity to warn the deer of what's coming. They'll know soon enough! Accordingly, within the month before open season — mid-October to mid-November, in my country — I may give certain targeted areas the once-over very lightly, slipping quietly across them, upwind, just once, checking trails and clearings for tracks and evaluating fall deer foods abundance and distribution. The delicacy called for in such work at this time of year can't be exaggerated; I should already know all I need to in order to hunt sensibly. These autumn forays are just a quick check for unexpected changes in movement patterns.

Finally, during the actual hunting season, I continue my low-profile scouting, usually making a short circle around my stand after I leave it for the morning. These brief sorties are only to check for new rubs and scrapes near the stand, to keep track of the onset of the rut, and to monitor changes in traffic volume on familiar trails. The less disturbance created during the hunting season itself, the better, especially near established stands or blinds.

By now it should be obvious why late winter and/or springtime is the most critical scouting period of the year. Being shortly after the end of a hunting season, it yields the most accurate picture of deer movement patterns during the season, as well as some information about the surviving bucks. If you plan to hunt a completely unfamiliar area for the first time next season, you may have to do more intensive autumn scouting to locate the mast, fruits, and other favored food sources, but, otherwise, get it all done by June. After that, intrude in the woods as little as possible until it's time to tote a rifle (read: bow, shotgun, muzzleloader, whatever's legal).

That's Scouting Lite, and it pays big dividends.

CHAPTER NINE

MAN-MADE MOVEMENT

Deer drives are not a hunting tradition in my neck of the woods. I remember taking part in occasional drives in east Texas, but we had nobody with the experience to organize and direct a drive correctly, so our efforts were seldom productive. Drives appear to be traditional nowhere in the U.S., in fact, except in the northeastern states and parts of the upper midwest. In those areas, driving has been honed to a fine art. Under the direction of a veteran hunt master, certain "drives" — well-known routes through specific areas with established standers' positions — have been producing venison for decades, and have acquired their own histories and names.

The Mystique of the Drive

"We'll do Big Hollow tomorrow morning," a drive captain may say, "looks like the wind'll be right and we have the extra men we need for that one. Oughta be a big buck in there, and he'll probably come out right on top, just east of that big bluff, just like Horace's, three years ago. Let's see — we need somebody there who can shoot quick. Billy, you know that old, lightning-split beech tree? You stand right there, and I'll bet you get a shot!"

The Big Hollow drive has probably been made so often that the hunters know each driver's route through the terrain, all the nooks and coves in which the deer usually hide, and their escapeways. This kind of drive, in which I have participated in New England, is usually made by groups of hunters who know each other and the countryside well, and it is an impressive team effort. If the big buck is taken, every man in camp will feel that he had an important part in the hunt, no matter whose shot fells the buck.

In many cases, these camps drive deer because that's the way it has always been done there, and the knowledge and skills have been passed down by their fathers and grandfathers. They do not resort to the drive because they know no other way to get a deer, but because this is the *best* way they know, and they enjoy the camaraderie, excitement, and suspense of the drive. Driving is an active hunt, rather than a passive one, with a clearly-defined end, and the hunters can follow the progress and events of the effort by ear. The direction and distance of shots and shouts heighten the suspense as they try to guess who got the shot and whether he got the buck. For readers unfamiliar with this mode of hunting whitetails, I should add that it is not only the standers who get the shots; many hunters get their deer while acting as drivers, too.

The General

Truthfully, although I have participated, I am no expert on driving deer, at least on these group drives. I do know something about the smaller, specialized drives which will be discussed a little farther along, but about large-group drives the thing I know for sure is that the campaign needs an experienced hunt captain to organize the whole effort. He must know the terrain intimately and how different winds lie across it, and how long the drive will take. He should be in charge of placing the standers and directing the drivers. He is the general, and leader-

The author shot this fine buck, the heaviest of his career, on a stop-and-go drive.

ship is among his more important qualifications. A good captain is not only key to a drive's success, but, even more important, to the safety of all participants.

Pushing Bush

Large group drives are best suited to big woods. Small, isolated woodlots and thickets, such as are found on the prairies of western Canada, are a different kind of challenge, calling for different tactics. This game, locally called "pushing bush," works well with a few men, and I've worked it with just two. A new tracking snow is a asset in this pastime, when a big buck's fresh tracks point to a certain patch of bush. Then two or three guns go around and cover most of the edges of the patch while their companions push through the thicket. It may be discovered, when the pushers break out, that the buck hadn't stopped in that particular bush, after all, and the party then follows the track on toward the next cover.

If the buck is in the bush, one of two things can happen: he may come out ahead of the drivers, or he may stay in the bush. If he comes out, the riflemen may miss him or they may hit him. If he lies low in the bush, he may succumb to a second pushing effort, or he may slip away while the hunters are wondering where he went. Even in a half-acre thicket, I've seen a buck elude two drivers, neither of whom laid an eyeball on him as they passed through the cover. It was impossible that they could have passed more than about 30 or 40 yards from the deer, at most, yet neither saw him. We went back through the bush and, lo and behold!, he went bouncing out the far side, waving his tail at us like a great, white, wagging middle finger!

The Whitetail Buck at His Best

How do they do that? It may seem impossible, but a white-tail buck can make himself practically invisible in cover you wouldn't think could hide a house cat. He can simply lie down and stretch his chin out on the ground, with a few bushes around him, and I guarantee you will not see him as long as he remains motionless. He can also walk in such a low crouch that his belly almost drags the ground, seeming to glide across the forest floor like a great antlered snake!

And he has the nerves of a cat burglar. He will stand like a statue as long as he believes himself unseen, and permit an armed man to walk past within 10 or 15 yards. Make eye-contact with him at a time like that, though, and he will literally explode in your face like a brown-and-white grenade!

I remember a guide in Alberta walking through thick bush with an autoloading shotgun, unleashing a 12-gauge blast into the air every few steps. Not only did the buck we sought stay put, but even his doe lay low until the guide had passed and then broke out behind him, distracting both of us from the buck's departure from the opposite side.

In my experience, actually to drive an old whitetail buck anywhere he doesn't want to go falls somewhere between unlikely and unthinkable. My favorite kind of drive simply encourages — rather than forces — him to move, and then allows his own instincts to betray him. I'll explain.

Two-Man Drives

Something called a "tandem drive" is performed by only two hunters, preferably two who know each other well

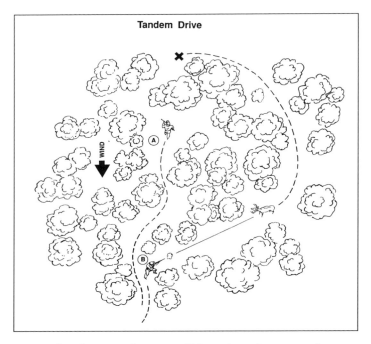

Tandem Drive

In a tandem drive, two hunters still-hunt through cover on the same route, with one far enough in front of the other to just keep in touch visually. Hunter A jumps buck at X, which circles, unaware of Hunter B, and Hunter B takes the shot while buck is still intent on his partner.

enough to develop a deep mutual trust. They slip along together, upwind, slowly and quietly as though still-hunting, through medium-heavy cover. One man walks about 100 yards or so ahead of the other, the spacing between them varying with the thickness of the cover. The trailing man closes up when he is not quite able to see his partner ahead of him and drops back a little when he can. He must know where the lead hunter is at all times.

The tandem drive is designed to take advantage of the fact that bucks, upon detecting the approach of a slow-moving hunter, tend to slink out of his path and then immediately circle back in behind him to pick up his scent. Their attention is riveted on the man they know about, and they may all but run over the one they don't! The leading hunter has the same chance to get a shot as while still-hunting alone through the same cover, but the

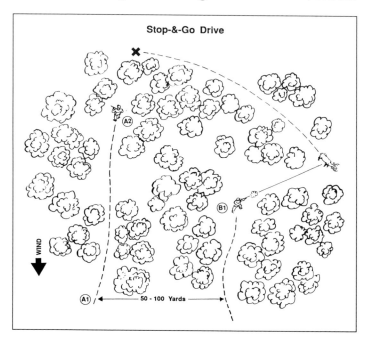

Stop-&-Go Drive

WIND

50 - 100 Yards

Hunters in a stop-and-go drive leapfrog each other on parallel courses, taking turns standing still and advancing. Hunter A stopped at A1 while partner B caught up and moved ahead to B1, where B waited as A still-hunter forwards to A2, where he spooked the buck bedded at X. Focussed on Hunter A, the buck overlooks B and offers a shot as he begins his circle.

trailing hunter always gets most of the best chances, so the partners should switch positions at intervals.

Obviously, for the sake of safety, the trailing hunter must be disciplined enough to take shots only off to the side, approximately at right angles to the line of march. That's where he'll first see the bucks, anyway.

A variation is the "stop-and-go" drive, also executed by two hunters. They still-hunt on parallel tracks, from 50 to 150 yards apart. Their spacing must permit them to keep track of one another visually, at least from time to time. One man stands still while the other advances, slowly and quietly, for 100 or 200 steps. Then he stops and stands motionless, watching, while his partner moves forward. The partner advances to a point abreast of his stationary buddy, and then another 100 or so yards ahead before stopping and waiting for the second man to catch up and take the lead.

This mode of driving requires a certain understanding of one's partner and his ways in the woods, but the rapport between good friends can become almost uncanny. It also requires an iron-bound determination never to risk a shot, however tempting, toward his partner's side. The rule is that neither man shoots at any deer at which he would not fire if the two of them were walking side by side.

Like the tandem drive, stop-and-go driving depends upon a buck's being unaware of a second hunter, and exposing himself to the second man in his effort to evade the first. It's a much more successful tactic in big woods, in my experience, than any possible two-man variation of conventional driving.

Said conventional driving can work very well with only two participants, however, when you know where a disturbed deer is probably going in advance. Then one man sets up there, and the other goes and disturbs the deer. Easy pickings!

Well, not necessarily, because nobody really knows what a whitetail deer is going to do when he sets out to duck a hunter. Nevertheless, a situation presents itself now and then in which the odds that a buck will do a certain thing are good enough to try a one-man drive. An example is a buck spotted where he might be pushed along a narrow line of brush and trees, perhaps lining a drainage in otherwise open country. If not crowded too hard, a buck usually opts to remain inside the cover rather than expose himself on either side. I did say "usually," because a whitetail buck is certainly bold enough to make a break for it in the open if he suspects a trap. The trick is to keep him from suspecting, by keeping out of sight and downwind while moving quickly into position. Such operations are often spur-of-the-moment improvisations and the trap must be set up fast. Sometimes they work and sometimes they don't, but drives of this kind have produced some fun and a few fine bucks for my friends and me.

The Circle Drive

Another two-man driving tactic for big woods is sometimes called the "circle drive." In this operation, the two hunters walk together to a stand. One occupies it and the other walks away, but not in a straight line. Instead, he makes a circle with the stand at its center, and then describes another, larger circle, and so on, following an ever-widening spiral. Depending on the thickness of the cover, his first circle should be perhaps 100 yards from the stand, the second 200, and so on out to about a quarter of a mile.

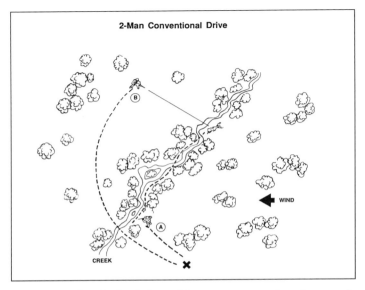

2-Man Conventional Drive

WIND

CREEK

Hunter A pushes the buck through heavy cover growing along creek, while his partner B circles downwind to locate a break in the tree-line where the buck will be exposed as he crosses. The hunters gamble that the buck will be reluctant to leave cover for the open country on each side, as long as he never senses Hunter B's maneuver.

This exploits two weaknesses in a whitetail's defenses: first, he can't count, so he may not realize that one hunter remained in the stand when the other departed. Second, he's single-minded, and can become so intent on evading the moving man that he may expose himself to the stander. I read about the circle drive many years ago in an obscure book on deer hunting, and scoffed at the idea. Then one day I accompanied a companion to show him the location of a tree in which I had a platform stand. In leaving, I decided to return to the vehicle by another route. I walked straight away, far enough that I wouldn't disturb the woods around my friend's location too badly, and then swung a radius of perhaps 150 yards from the stand. Before I'd taken another 50 steps, my friend's rifle roared and I heard the bullet slap home hard! It turned out that the fine buck he'd shot had been trotting back toward the stand from the direction in which I was heading. Backtracking him, I could see that I had, unconsciously, executed a perfect circle drive for that stand. The whole affair caused my doubts about this version of two-man driving to evaporate, and I've used it repeatedly since that day. Don't underestimate the circle drive!

There are almost infinite variations of these and other man-driving patterns, suggested by different terrain

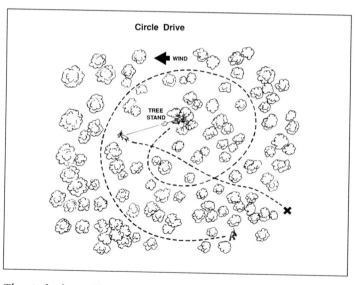

The circle drive allows a single driver to stir up deer within a few hundred yards of his partner's stand. Again, deer seeking to elude the walking man by circling behind him or running across the circle may be seen from the stand.

features, conditions, and the resources available to the hunting group. One asset not yet discussed is a pack of deer hounds.

Driving with Dogs

Hound-driving is an ancient sport, probably one of mankind's oldest hunting methods. For most hounds-men, breeding, training, and running the hounds is the real sport, and the deer — or other big game — are mainly an object on which to exercise and with which to justify the time and expense of keeping a pack. That is not intended to be derogatory, nor to imply that legal hound-hunting is in any way unfair, unsportsmanlike, or dishonorable. It is, rather, my explanation for giving little space in this text to a pastime of intense importance to a great many passionate hunters. Hounding is legal mostly in the coastal lowlands of the south Atlantic seaboard and the Gulf of Mexico, but it appears to be dying out. In swampy east Texas, for example, hounding was a major sport in my boyhood, but the state has recently banned it entirely, after a two-year study on the impact of dog hunting on the whitetail herd. I have participated in hound hunts for deer, and find them interesting but only distantly related to deer hunting. Hounds are simply a different game, but must be mentioned here as an undeniably effective means of moving whitetail deer.

There are other ways of causing deer to come to the hunter, besides driving. Most have been or will be mentioned in greater detail elsewhere, including grunt-calling, horn-rattling, and decoying. Still another is baiting.

Baiting Whitetails

At this point, I suppose there is no more controversial topic in American deer hunting. Feelings run high on both sides. Hunting deer over bait is lawful in 21 states, according to a recent survey. That includes most of the states having significant whitetail populations east of the great plains. In another 12 states, feeding deer is allowed, but all feed must be removed from a hunting area prior to the open season. Baiting, therefore, is a widespread and legal hunting practice across the eastern two-thirds or so of the U.S. You must check your local regulations, of course, before hunting by this — or any other — method.

I do not intend here to solve what many see as an ethical problem in deer hunting, nor even to take sides. I was raised and received all my early hunting training in a state in which baiting has always been acceptable, but

I was nearly 30 years old, and had probably shot 25 or 30 bucks, before I ever saw deer eat corn. Baiting was simply not a part of my early whitetail curriculum. I do recall hunting over agricultural crops, especially winter oats, long before I ever saw food put out to lure deer to hunting blinds. Few of even the most vehement opponents of baiting, I notice, seem to object to sitting over a soybean field, although the distinction is not evident.

Although I rarely use bait in my own hunting, I have no strong bias on the ethical question in either direction. If it's legal and it suits your personal style, I don't care if you put out chocolate eclairs for the whitetails, much less a little corn, or sweet potatoes, carrots, apples, or whatever! If you don't like it, don't do it. Nor do I perceive an overwhelming moral superiority in hunting near standing crops, either wild or domestic, over hunting near a bait pile. I do know that we hunters need no more intra-fraternal sniping over imaginary distinctions between types of hunting weapons, methods, equipment, seasons, or whatever. The anti-hunters and animals-rights fanatics lift their glasses to toast each new example of such stupidity on our part. Every attack you launch against your brother hunters, as long as they're legal under the laws of your state, is another ax-stroke at the base of the mighty oak called Sport Hunting for Common Folks, which has grown only on this continent. But enough of preaching.

Baiting whitetails is legal in large sectors of the U.S., and it works. But it's hardly a "sure thing," as most people seem to believe. Does and young bucks come readily to bait, but mature bucks are a different matter. In my observation, the heavy-headed old boys show up at the bait pile, if at all, after dark. Some never come. The buck hunter's best hope is that a doe in estrus will be attracted

The Canadian small-group driving tactic called "pushin' bush" ben-
efits from a light, fresh snowfall to show which bush should be
pushed. This track of a big whitetail buck points like a neon sign to
the animal's probable hideout.

to the bait while she's being followed by a big buck. However it works out, baiting moves deer around. Even when you do not hunt within sight of the bait or the clover patch, you will benefit from the spontaneous deer movement generated by the artificial feeding sites in the vicinity.

Variations

Such sites can be locally ingenious. Hard as it may be to believe, whitetails love prickly pear cactus, and make it their most-utilized plant in regions where it's abundant. Some friends of mine in south Texas once ran a big agricultural shredder over a dense patch or "flat" of prickly pear, with the cutting blade set about 18 inches above the ground. They told me that the deer were so attracted to the smell of the freshly-chopped cactus that they actually came out of the brush and followed the tractor as it worked. Later, I shot a very big buck out of one of those shredded pear flats.

Now, the question is: did I shoot him over bait? The natural food that attracted him was not planted or cultivated, and was a normal part of his everyday diet. The shredder merely made it more available to the deer, and did not permanently damage the resource. How about it, you ethicists? How is hunting over a natural food like cactus different from hunting in a grove of white oaks in a good acorn year? Or knocking down a few apples in an abandoned orchard before taking a stand?

Tricky questions; don't offer a smug answer without thinking twice!

Just as there's more than one way to skin a cat, there's more than one way to force — or entice — a whitetail deer to get out of bed and move!

CHAPTER TEN

STANDING AND SITTING
(AND SOMETIMES LYING!)

Some seem to feel that there's nothing more to stand-hunting than simply going out in the woods and sitting down to wait for a deer to amble by. It gives me pleasure to disabuse them of such a silly notion. Stand hunting is quite an art, and is closely connected to our theme in this volume of whitetail movement. The Brothers Wensel, Gene and Barry, are scheduled to contribute a volume on the subject in this *WHITETAIL SECRETS* series, but stand-hunting and deer movement are sufficiently intertwined to justify a few paragraphs here, as well.

As I pointed out before, deer do not move at random. It isn't easy to figure out what an animal is up to at any moment, but, if he's on the move, you can take it for granted that he's headed for a known destination, and for a reason. Radio telemetry studies indicate that there are places in a deer's home range which the deer never visits; obviously, a stand in one of those is in the wrong place. Part of the art of stand hunting is in locating a stand, not only in one of the right places, but in the very best place available at the moment.

Here the author uses a commercial ladder stand to replace an ancient nailed-up tree stand, pieces of which can be seen in the tree behind him. This has evidently been a good place to hunt for many years.

Fabricated Stands are New

During the first 19 years of my whitetail hunting career, I never saw a fabricated deer-hunting stand, either commercial or home-made. I do remember a rusty, junked Mercury coupe (about 1935 vintage) sitting on the edge of a field, from which some hunting was done, especially on bitter, windy, or rainy days. It remained in place year-'round, the deer ignored it, and it made a very comfortable blind . . . but old cars don't count. All the other "deer stands" around the old Fonville camp were nothing more than conveniently located tree trunks which happened to overlook well-known whitetail crossings or runways. They all had names, but the name designated the crossing more than the tree. To hunt that crossing, you simply sat down on the ground with your back against the tree trunk. On some crossings there was a preferred tree for morning hunts and another for afternoon hunts. There was no cover or concealment around these "stands"; it would have interfered with swinging a rifle. And there were no camouflaged hunting clothes in those days, either. You sat out in the open, and you sat *still*, until it was time to raise the rifle. Sitting really still — like, *totally motionless* — is a skill of the really motivated younger person. Little kids can't do it, and neither can people of my present age class, at least not for hour after hour. My non-hunting mother once sat on a deer stand with me for an afternoon, when I was thirtysomething, and reported that she had to check my breathing from time to time to make sure I wasn't dead! She said I didn't move a muscle for so long that it made her

Modern camouflage is so good that ground blinds are hardly needed by a hunter who knows how to sit still.

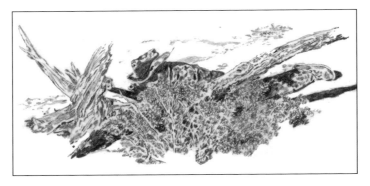

nervous. I was pleased when she said that. Still-sitting was a point of pride with me in those days.

It remains a valuable knack for any deer hunter, but is not as critical as before the days of camo and various other modern modes of concealment in the woods. Some of the new proprietary camouflage patterns today are so amazingly good that you can actually get away with a little judicious movement, even in the open with whitetails within range. In fact, when stand-hunting on the ground these days I hardly feel the need for any kind of blind when togged out in one of the newest versions of Bushlan, RealTree Universal, Mossy Oak, or All-Purpose TreBark, provided my background is right. Commercial portable ground blinds in many styles are sold, but I prefer just a few sticks and tufts of local natural materials. That, plus a suit of today's state-of-the-art camo (including coverings for face and hands, of course) and a little shade to sit in, is enough to be effectively invisible, if one can sit still.

To prevent readers from suspecting that the last phrase in this chapter's title is meant to reflect on the truthfulness of deer hunters, I should tell here about taking nice bucks on two different occasions, not by sitting or standing, but by literally lying in wait for them — on my belly. In each case the deer was known to cross a certain *sendero* regularly on which I could find no good place to sit or to install any sort of stand or blind with the wind right. So I dragged a handy log out into the opening and lay down flat on my stomach behind it, my pre-aimed rifle resting across the log. I wore full camo and tried to be as motionless as the log. No part of me, my equipment, or my log stood more than 12 or 15 inches above the earth. Both bucks saw me instantly when they stepped out of the brush, one at less than 25 yards. But apparently nothing about an old log seemed threatening, and they were still staring curiously when my bullets struck.

Tree Stands And Tripods

Where suitable trees grow, tree stands are available in a hundred styles — climbing, chain-on, portable, semi-portable, semi-permanent, ladder-style, everything except self-levitating. Where trees are absent, poorly-located, or of improper size or shape to support a conventional manufactured stand, a swivel seat mounted atop a set of portable legs suggests itself. I believe the first homemade examples of this idea appeared in Texas back in the late '40s or '50s, when hunters began to mount iron tractor seats on wooden step-ladders and paint the whole rig green. It was a handy idea, especially where the "trees" were more shrubs than trees, and it quickly appeared in a wide variety of commercial forms, typified today by the generic portable tripod stand, topped by a plastic boat seat, weighing between 30 and 50 pounds complete and perhaps folding or telescoping into a more manageable package. Some models come with gun rests or without (for bowhunters), some with camo covers (or without, also for bowhunters), and one even comes with a universal swivel arm to which your video camcorder can be attached, so you can get better footage of the bucks you *didn't* shoot! Tripod stands in any these modes are widely applicable and highly practical.

So, at last we have the equipment that we lacked (but didn't know we needed, or what we were missing) during my early years. The crucial question, however, hasn't changed: where to put the stand?

The tractor-seat-on-a-stepladder makeshift portable stands of the '50s quickly evolved into sophisticated, lightweight, collapsible tripods which do not depend upon a climbable tree growing at exactly the right spot.

Stand Location

That, of course, is what all that scouting in Chapter Eight was all about: finding where in the woods the deer are "using," and analyzing the movement patterns around those places. Setting up over such obvious attractions as agricultural fields or, in dry country, waterholes, calls for little genius, but those movement patterns require some study. It goes without saying, of course, that the stand location must always be downwind from the field or waterhole or game trail, but it pays to give some thought to where the animals may be coming from. If that turns out to be a bed ground that's fairly close to and downwind of the feeding area, as it often will be in flat terrain, you may have to wait for the wind to change before setting up there. Most experts I know actually prefer to hunt the trails themselves, rather than the food plots or fields, because the direction and timing of the deer movement there is a little easier to predict. Also, mature bucks tend to move more confidently along trails through cover, especially in daylight.

The flexibility of tripods permits adjustment of their locations as deer movement patterns change with the season.

Where a stand is positioned depends upon what you expect the buck you intend to shoot from it to be doing. That may depend on the structure of the open season, weapons, and other hunting regulations in your state. If you're in a shotguns-only state or during a muzzleloader or bowhunting subseason, you probably won't erect the stand where you might see a trophy at 250 yards. If the rut doesn't fall within your local open season, then you'll most likely be relying on deer movement motivated by feeding and/or watering to bring your prize within range of the stand.

You will not erect a stand on whitetail bedding areas, of course, except perhaps in a rare situation where you're trying to catch a totally nocturnal buck just as he arrives

The famed "Texas tower" elevated blinds evolved from platforms built in windmill towers where no suitable stand trees exist. This is a two-man model.

in his bedroom at dawn, after a night on the town. The trouble is that bed grounds are not all that small and specific, and a buck may just lie down anywhere he happens to feel safe. I've had a buck walk in and lie down just a few feet from the scrape I was hunting, and I've often had bucks bed down in plain sight in the middle of a field or other feeding area. In steeper terrain whitetails seem pretty uniformly to prefer high ground for resting places, where daytime thermals can bring to their nostrils the scent of predators approaching from below. But in level to gently rolling country, which probably takes in most of America's prime whitetail habitat, bedding areas are not so easy to pinpoint. Backtrail the main runways to find bedding areas. When you notice the main trail fork-

Is shredding naturally-growing prickly pear cactus to attract whitetails "baiting"? If not, what is it? If so, is it unethical? The whole baiting controversy must be solved — and soon — if we are to present a united front to the animal-rightists.

ing, and then forking again and again, and then petering out, you're in the area, and deer beds should be fairly easily found in shady spots nearby.

For that matter, in many parts of the whitetail range, it's not so easy to nail down feeding areas, either. Deer feed on so many kinds of plants and shrubs that they might find a snack almost anywhere in their home ranges. Merely observing trailside feeding activity doesn't mean that you've discovered the secret key to what the deer will do next.

If anybody ever tells you that he knows what a whitetail buck will do or exactly where he will be during the peak of the rut, either he's lying or he arrived on the last UFO! Bucks' activities during this frenzied time are so erratic that they hardly even make sense to the buck, much less to a hunter. Besides which, bucks are individuals exhibiting a complete spectrum of preferences and reactions. Some like to stick pretty close to home, even during the rut, while others ramble far and wide. I once "lost" a big buck I spotted the weekend after Labor Day, only to find him in January, a full three miles as the crow flies from where he first appeared. The season, needless to say, was no longer open at the time of this second coming.

Hunt the Does

The solution to this Rutting Buck Puzzle is actually quite logical: *hunt the does!* Nobody can predict the movements of a rutting buck, except to say that he will go wherever the does are. If you can find the right scrape, of course, a high probability exists that the buck — or at least *a* buck — will return to that place, sometime,

looking the same area, never hunting from the same one twice. This can have the advantage of different places to sit for different wind directions, but it also keeps the deer guessing about where the possible danger is, and helps delay or avoid the burn-out of any one stand. Such multiple stands, and rotating their use, are first-rate refinements — if you don't mind the investment in equipment, and, more cogently, if you hunt where you can leave your equipment in the woods without having it stolen. Sadly, this means that we're talking mostly about private property.

With the same reservation, we may as well say a few words about the so-called *lay-down* stand, a device I use often and very effectively. It amounts to a lightweight tripod that is left where it's wanted for hunting but laid down on the ground when not in use. The practice eliminates the possibility of damage to the tripod from being blown over by a wind gust while vacant — or the bother of rigging guy-wires to prevent that. More important, it leaves nothing standing to alert the deer herd to human activity in the area. In short, a given buck will see the stand in place for the first time when he first walks into view while a hunter is on it. The deer will notice the strange object instantly, of course, but it will be too late by then if the hunter wants him. Erecting the typical portable tripod is quick, quiet, and easy, as is lowering it when leaving. By taking pains to keep two of the three legs exactly in place during both operations, the hunter's view will be identical on each visit. This can be important, since many tripods are employed exactly for the reason that no suitable tree for a stand happens to be situated where a hunter can have precisely the vista he needs.

The Substitute Dummy

If a tripod is to be left standing between hunts for some reason, it must be guyed against blowdowns, and there is another gimmick that I can't resist mentioning. It is the practice of leaving some sort of dummy which suggests the shape of a man in the seat while the hunter is absent. I've used burlap potato sacks stuffed with such things as grass or styrofoam chips, with a rope tied to form a constriction at the "neck". Be warned that a bungee cord or other means of lashing the dummy in place is necessary to prevent wind or birds of prey from displacing it. It will take the local deer a while, but they will eventually accustom themselves to the unmoving presence of that mass up there on the seat, and will not notice when it is exchanged for a similar mass with a rifle lying across its lap!

This is a neat trick, producing a truly eerie sensation of invisibility as you sit on the stand in plain sight and watch deer and other wildlife go about their business close by without a second glance at you. My wiseacre

This grand whitetail — the best of Wootters' more than 200 bucks — was taken while stand hunting.

favorite hunting companion — and wife — insists on calling the stuffed sack the "substitute dummy," but the results are worth a little ridicule.

Stands — whether elaborate tower blinds, ground blinds of brush, tree stands, tripods, or merely well-placed tree trunks — exist to overlook places and trails where whitetails move, which is why this chapter was essential to a book on deer movement.

CHAPTER ELEVEN

CONCLUSION

If this book is to have any lasting value, it will have to give a hunter who reads it something to think about. This is more important, in fact, than actually teaching him something he didn't know before. Hunting the American whitetail deer in fair chase is, perhaps surprisingly, a quite cerebral pastime. A big-game hunter may climb his way to a Rocky Mountain goat, or walk his way to a mule deer, or pay his way to a record-book elk . . . but he *thinks* his way to a big, mature whitetail buck.

We hear a lot about "luck" in whitetail hunting — how this guy got lucky on the new state record or that one had "beginner's luck" on a book deer. I'll tell you a secret: the longer I study the whitetail scene, the more I'm tempted to conclude that "luck" is something invented by losers to explain the success of those who are better than they themselves are at whatever is being discussed! "Beginner's luck" is often a matter of an inexperienced hunter making, through ignorance, exactly the right — and often unorthodox — move at just the right time. That's not, in my view, quite the same thing. A hunter who consistently fills his tags with big antlers, year after year, is not lucky; he's good. There's very little luck, in the sense of blind good fortune, in deer hunting.

Furthermore, the whitetail deer may be the only species of North American big game of which the mere expenditure of money, energy, and time cannot guarantee a record-book trophy, at least in a truly fair-chase context. More than any other, this species demands a fourth ingredient: knowledge.

Successful deer hunting is usually not physically demanding, as mountain game can be, but it is nevertheless hard work. Not only does it require a great deal of patience and time in scouting and setting up, but one has to think a lot . . . and thinking is some of the hardest work there is!

It may be that the greatest asset a deer hunter has is not his firearm or his camouflage or his bait pile, but the unique power of his creative imagination!

Every extraordinarily successful whitetail hunter of my long experience has been a man of imagination.

An understanding of what makes whitetails move — and where, when, and how — helped the author collect this mature 10-pointer after watching the deer for several seasons.

None of them took the whitetail deer for granted (very easy to do . . . and easy to regret!), and none of them ever allowed the deer to take them for granted! Without exception, these legendary hunters have evolved their own distinctive theories of whitetail behavior and tactics for whitetail hunting. They read, listened politely to "experts," and then went out and asked the deer, learning from the penultimate experts on whitetail behavior, the animals themselves. These men — and a few women, too — do things differently. They build on the experience of those who taught them, and then push the envelope for themselves, experimenting with new approaches and ideas. Their techniques never cease evolving, because they never cease challenging their own assumptions. They haunt the woods, always watching and wondering, noticing details about the whitetail lifestyle and trying to find new fits between observations and orthodoxy. Where they cannot, all the legendary hunters I've known have thrown out the orthodoxy and boldly proceeded on their own novel concepts.

Such men and women, by the way, will be the authors of all the volumes in this WHITETAIL SECRETS series to come, which is why the project is so exciting. The opportunity to compare the opinions of so many different experts on certain subjects, such as stand-hunting or scouting, as well as their hunting philosophies, may become the series' single most priceless feature.

In my own extensive writing and lecturing about hunting the wily whitetail, I've always stressed this: we may not be very successful in "patterning" the buck, but we must at all costs prevent him from patterning us! That means pitching him a curve, a woodlands change-up, playing him a different tune, showing him something he hasn't seen before. It's all too easy to get locked into a

The finest buck yet collected from their ranch was taken by the author's wife, Jeannie, co-owner of Los Cuernos, after a meticulous, week-long scouting project. What moved him? The rut, of course!

hunting rut, doing everything the way our grandfather or uncle always did it. That's not only obsolescent; it's boring, and, above all, deer hunting shouldn't be boring!

Therefore I welcome innovation in the deer-hunting scene. In recent years alone the introduction of serious grunt-calling and the use of decoys, to name just a couple, have greatly livened up my hours in the woods. My present opinions on these two subjects, too, are today almost opposite to my earliest reactions to them.

On the other hand, in my judgement it's all too easy to get caught up in gimmickry and gadgetry. Whitetail hunters are no more immune to these diseases than golfers or — heaven forbid! — bass fishermen. Some of these new products are actually useful, and some are fun, but none can replace a thorough, basic understanding of the whitetail deer and the world he lives in. They're like icing on a cake; useful refinements, but they can never substitute for a hunter's skill and knowledge. The most successful deer hunter will always be the person who knows most about the animal's needs, priorities, character, habits, and responses. That's why the discussion of whitetail movements — what motivates them and what suppresses them — presented in this book is important to anyone who wants to be a whitetail hunter.

The slightest glimmer of just one new idea — perhaps based on something I've said here — can revolutionize your whole approach to deer hunting. I remember the flash of insight I received years ago while reading Robert Ardrey's book, *THE TERRITORIAL IMPERATIVE*; suddenly my hunter's mind shifted gears, and, in a twinkling, I visualized the outlines of my theory of whitetail breeding territories as distinguished from home ranges. A new way of thinking about whitetails and the many ways to hunt them may be the most significant lesson and legacy from this book or one of the 23 others to follow.

INDEX

Note: Bold page numbers indicate illustrations or photos.

Shooting, 121
  See also Hunting
Sightings
  afternoon, 83
  in database, 81–83
  duplicate, 83–85
  during rut, **108**, 119
  evening, **47**, 125
  morning, 37, **47**
  See also Records
Sky conditions, 88, **89**, 92
  See also Weather
Solunar Tables, 101–103
Spring, scouting in, 130–136
Stalking, 121–123
  vs. active hunting, 9–10
Stand burn-out, **52**, 55–57, 169–170
Stand-hunting, 9, 157
  for behavior observation, 39
  during rut, 115–116
  at midday, 73–75
  time periods for, 11
Stands
  dummies in, **168**, 171–173
  ladder stand, **158**
  lay-down stand, 170
  locating, 157, **158**, 163–164, 173
  stand burn-out, **52**, 55–57,
  169–170
  tree stands, 161–162
  tripod, 161–162, **168**, 170
  See also Blinds
Still-hunting
  during rut, 116
  rewards of, 10–13, **14**
  time periods for, 11
  vs. passive hunting, 9–10
Still-sitting, 159–160, 161
Summer, scouting in, 133–135
Survival
  for fawns, 66
  in post-rut recovery, 65–66

Tarsal glands, 107, 113, **115**, 119
  See also Bucks; Rut
Temperature, effect on whitetails,
  89–91, **90**, 92, 93
  See also Weather
Territory
  for breeding, **58**, **70**, 111, 129
  identifying, 45–46
  vs. home range, 19–22, 179
  See also Home range
Texas camp, 35, **36**

Topographical maps
  for locating cover, 59
  for locating game trails, 131
  See also Geography
Trails
  barriers to, 132–133, **134**
  to bedding areas, 166–167
  buck corridors, **126**, 131–132, 163
  game trails, **126**, 131–132
  hunting from, 71–73
  in hunting season, 58–59
  observing from stand, 56–57
  scouting for, 123–127, 131–133
  scrapes on, 129
  See also Bedding area; Scouting

Water
  and movement, 40–41, 45, **46**, 164
  anticipating bucks at, 37–38, **42**
  from forage, 45
  See also Forage
Waterholes
  hunting at, 45, 163
  scouting at, 125–127, 133
Weather
  effect on movement, 12, 13, 22,
    32–33, 41, 57, 61, 79–93
  humidity factor, 83
  predicted by whitetail, 87–88
  for scouting, 130–131
  sky conditions, 88
  temperature factor, 89–91, **90**
  See also Records
White cedar, as food source, 44
  See also Forage
Whitetail
  cyclical movement, 31
  digestive system, 42
  individuality, 15, 17
  migratory patterns, 22
  patterning, 30
  subspecies, 16–17
  See also Bucks; Does; Herd
Wind
  effect on tripods, 170, 171, 172
  effect on whitetails, **84**, 86–87, 125
  and stand locations, 163–164
  velocity effect, 91–93, **93**
  See also Barometric pressure;
    Weather
Winter
  deer movement in, 22, 32
  scouting in, 130–131, 135–136

Yards, winter movement to, 22, 32

WHITETAIL SECRETS
VOLUME ONE — WHITETAIL MOVEMENT

Black and white photography by John Wootters

Color photography by Mike Biggs:
Pages 6, 18, 34, 50, 62, 78, 94, 104

Color photography by Craig Boddington: Pages 120, 138

Color photography by John Wootters:
Frontispiece, Pages 156, 174

Illustrated by David Baer

Designed by Donna M. Wright

Text composed in Berkeley Oldstyle by
AeroType, Inc., Amherst, New Hampshire

Color Separations and Film prepared by
Charles Hurley

Printed and Bound by
Quebecor Printing, Kingsport, Tennessee

Text sheets are acid-free Warren Flo Book by
S. D. Warren Company

Endleaves are Rainbow Parchment by
Ecological Fibers, Inc.

Cover material is Taratan II Bonded Leather by
Cromwell